CITYSPOTS
KIEV

Tom Burgess

Written by Tom Burgess
Original photography by Tony Gervis
Front cover photograph courtesy of www.photolibrary.com

Produced by 183 Books
Design/layout/maps: Chris Lane and Lee Biggadike
Editorial/project management: Stephen York

Published by Thomas Cook Publishing
A division of Thomas Cook Tour Operations Limited
PO Box 227, Units 15/16, Coningsby Road
Peterborough PE3 8SB, United Kingdom
email: books@thomascook.com
www.thomascookpublishing.com
+44 (0) 1733 416477

First edition © 2006 Thomas Cook Publishing
Text © 2006 Thomas Cook Publishing
Maps © 2006 Thomas Cook Publishing
ISBN-13: 978-1-84157-583-4
ISBN-10: 1-84157-583-6
Project Editor: Kelly Anne Pipes
Production/DTP: Steven Collins

Printed and bound in Spain by GraphyCems

CONTENTS

INTRODUCING KIEV

Introduction 6
When to go 8
Urban weirdness.........................14
History 16
Lifestyle 18
Culture 22

MAKING THE MOST OF KIEV

Shopping 28
Eating & drinking 32
Entertainment & nightlife 38
Sport & relaxation 42
Accommodation 44
The best of Kiev 50
Something for nothing 54
When it rains 56
On arrival 58

THE CITY OF KIEV

Central Kiev 70
Pechersk 90
Podil...100
Around Kiev...............................108

OUT OF TOWN TRIPS

Lviv (Lvov)...................................116
Odessa...128

PRACTICAL INFORMATION

Directory......................................138
Useful phrases 154
Emergencies 156

INDEX 158

MAP LIST

Kiev city map 62
Kiev transport map..................66
Central Kiev.................................71
Pechersk..91
Podil..101
Lviv (Lvov) 117
Odessa 129

SYMBOLS & ABBREVIATIONS

The following symbols are used throughout this book:

☎ telephone   **ⓦ** website address   **ⓐ** address
☻ opening times   **Ⓝ** public transport connections

The following symbols and abbreviations are used on the maps:
✈ Airport
bulv. *bulvar* boulevard
pl. *ploscha* square
pros. *prospekt* avenue
prov. *provulok* lane, minor street
vul. *vulitsia* street

Hotels and restaurants are graded by approximate price as follows:
H budget price   **HH** mid-range price   **HHH** expensive
HHH+ very expensive
The local currency is the Hryvnia (see page 143)

24-HOUR CLOCK

All times in this book are given in the 24-hour clock system used widely in Europe and in most international transport timetables.

◐ *Independence Square is the heart of downtown Kiev*

INTRODUCING
Kiev

Introduction

Kiev (Kyiv) is the capital and most important city in Ukraine, once part of the Russian empire and later the Soviet Union. It is a city that is changing fast – or maybe not. It is an interesting mix of old and new, modern and classic, East and West, good and bad. Visiting Kiev will not only be interesting, it could prove to be a bit of an adventure. After centuries of being dominated and persecuted, the indomitable Ukraine spirit is free at last, but it does not seem quite sure of how to handle its newly won freedom and independence.

On one hand Kiev is trying very hard to westernise and bring in much-needed investment capital, while still clinging to the Soviet-era bureaucracy and red tape that slow the process. While trying to update their infrastructure, the Kiev authorities are also rebuilding the historic sites, especially the churches. Many streets are lined with nondescript Soviet-style tenements, yet Kiev has more area of

⬤ *Ukraine is fast embracing all aspects of Western life, from mobile phones to McDonald's*

parkland per citizen than just about any other city in the world. The city puts on a bright rich facade for the tourists but underneath poverty is still rampant. The airport and train terminal are as modern as any in Europe, yet the bus station and roads in general are decrepit. A high percentage of the people use the internet, yet the telephone system is unreliable. The city has some of the finest restaurants in the world, yet the water is unsafe to drink. Ukrainians by nature are open, friendly and honest, yet they seem suspicious of everyone.

The present is an exciting time to visit, not only because the prices are low, but also because you can be witness to the many changes that are taking place. Kiev is already far ahead of its two Russian counterparts, Moscow and St Petersburg, in becoming a vital, modern city. Given the vast resources the country is blessed with, and the determination of a newly freed and well educated people, it is only a matter of time before Kiev is one of the world's most important cities, as well as a favourite tourist destination.

KIEV OR KYIV?

The city is still best known in the English-speaking world as Kiev, a spelling that dates back to when Ukraine (no longer 'the' Ukraine) was part of Russia, and because of its familiarity that is the name used throughout this book. The more correct transliteration these days, however, is Kyiv, and this version is coming into increasing use in the West. As it is closer to the Ukrainian name and has no association with the days of Russian domination, this is the romanised spelling that Ukrainians prefer.

When to go

SEASONS & CLIMATE

Far from the year-round frozen wasteland that many envisage, Kiev has four distinct seasons. Although the winter can be harsh, the other three seasons are at least pleasant, and summer temperatures can reach 30°C (86°F). Any period from the beginning of May to the middle of October is a good time to visit. The weather is warm to hot, with lots of sunshine. The fields and trees are green, and the markets are full of fresh fruits and vegetables.

Spring and autumn are generally quite short, although warm and mild. Perhaps the very best month is May. This is when the sun begins to shine in earnest, and when the flowers and trees start to bloom and put on their finest greenery. This is the month the citizens of Kiev like the best, and it is the time when the city begins to come alive after the winter. Harvest time is in October, when the fields around Kiev are at their most picturesque. Summer is generally hot, with long days and lots of sunshine. Many of the most colourful cultural festivals occur in summer, and the tourist facilities are open, so it is a good time to visit. However, few hotels and other buildings have air-conditioning, so you may want to consider visiting in months other than July and August.

Winter starts in early November, and there is snow on the ground from late November until mid-April. January and February are the worst months in which to visit, with only a few hours of dreary sunshine a day and temperatures rarely above 0°C (32°F). Little or no attempt is made to clear snow from the streets, so getting around is very difficult.

● *Summer brings all the citizens of Kiev out onto the streets*

ANNUAL CELEBRATIONS

Ukrainians celebrate their civic and religious holidays with great enthusiasm. The biggest is the Christmas–New Year celebration. Dates include, in order, the Catholic Christmas on 25 December, the Gregorian New Year on 1 January, the Orthodox Christmas on 7 January, and the Julian New Year on 14 January. The Gregorian New Year holiday became the most important in the country during the Soviet reign because emphasis on the 1 January detracted from any religious recognition of Orthodox Christmas on the 7th. Preparations begin weeks before the holidays start, with Christmas lights and Christmas trees put up on the main streets and seasonal music being played in public. The city virtually shuts down during this period, and everyone eats and drinks to excess. It is a bad time to do business or to be a tourist, so unless you are into this kind of debauchery it is a good time to avoid visiting, quite apart from the weather.

The Orthodox Christmas almost coincides with the celebration of Epiphany. This is traditionally celebrated as a religious event where the hardiest souls find it necessary to leap into the River Dnepr to celebrate the arrival of Christ. The more circumspect bring a bucket of water to the islands just off the Hydropark to be blessed by the patriarch of Kiev.

International Women's Day, 8 March, is celebrated much as the Western world celebrates Mother's Day, with gifts and cards being given to women of all ages. It is also a day when men are supposed to do the cooking and cleaning for the women in their life.

Easter is the most important religious holiday in Ukraine, with long church services and other rituals and public displays. Special

▶ *Many Ukrainian festivals are still based on the Orthodox Church calendar*

foods and elaborately decorated Easter eggs are prepared for blessing by the priests. People greet each other with '*Yisus Voskres*' (Christ is risen), and respond with '*Va Istynno Voskres*' (Truly, He is risen).

To coincide with the end of winter there are two major celebrations held in early May. Labour Day or May Day, 1–2 May, is a holdover from the Soviet era and features military parades and fireworks. A week later on 9 May, Victory Day, celebrating the winning of World War II, is held. Again, it is mostly a military show with more parades and fireworks.

Ivana Kupala (St John's Baptism) is held the first week of July. It originated as a pagan ritual in honour of summer, but mutated into a Christian holiday with the arrival of Orthodoxy. Its main objectives are spiritual cleansing through the use of fire and water. The biggest summer holiday is Ukrainian Independence Day (24 August), commemorating the split from Russia in 1991. Mammoth parades and long-winded political speeches are its hallmarks. The Great October Socialist Revolution Anniversary, on 7 November, celebrates the revolution that overthrew the Tsars; it has become a minor holiday since independence, and most businesses stay open.

Weekends are party time in downtown Kiev. The main street, Khreschatyk, is closed to traffic and becomes busy with buskers, food and souvenir sellers, shoppers and people just hanging out.

ANNUAL EVENTS

Many music and film festivals occur during the year in Kiev. The biggest challenge is in locating up-to-date information on these events before your visit. The following are the best publicised.

May

Kiev Days (Last weekend of May) This is the city's biggest and best street festival, drawing up to 50,000 visitors to partake of food, music and merriment in the capital, centred on the Andrew's Descent area. This is a time when Kiev really kicks up her heels and celebrates her heritage.

September
Chaiki Rock Festival (the first week of September) celebrates hard rock, soft rock, and anything that makes you feel young and want to party, at the Chaika Sport Complex. Expect huge, boisterous crowds.
Kiev International Music Festival (last week of September) All forms of music come together in this festival of concerts. Jazz, chamber, symphonic and choral concerts are all celebrated with gusto. A very special event if you are a student – concert tickets are free.

October
Kiev International Film Festival – Molodist (late October) This international festival for young and first-time filmmakers has been taking place since 1994 and draws high-profile names such as Roman Polansky and Jerzy Hoffman as guest speakers.
ⓦ www.molodist.com

PUBLIC HOLIDAYS
New Year's Day 1 Jan
Orthodox Christmas Day 7 Jan
International Women's Day 8 Mar
Labour Days 1–2 May
Victory Day 9 May
Constitution Day 28 June
Ukrainian Independence Day 24 Aug

Urban weirdness

It is not just tales of Baba Yaga the sorceress, a central figure in Ukrainian children's stories, or yarns about brave Cossack warriors that permeate the local folklore. For some reason, Kiev's city landmarks have accumulated a set of urban legends that vary from the almost plausible to the utterly ridiculous. In some cases the building alone is strange enough. Here are just a few.

Richard's Castle

There is a local belief that this 'medieval castle' once played host to Richard the Lionheart on his return from a crusade. However, the building didn't appear until 1904. Dimitriy Orlov, a local contractor at the time, decided that he wanted to build a house in the English neo-gothic style. When it was completed it was an astonishing sight, with pointed spires, battlements, a covered staircase and a wonderfully romantic English garden. But it was 700 years too late to be a stopping place for King Richard. ❷ 15 Andreyesky Spusk.

Diakova's disturbance

The building in question is one of the wings of the present-day Central Post Office. It was once inhabited by a rather eccentric woman known as Diakova. During the 1950s the city's newspapers carried a sensational story claiming that cushions, blankets and bed sheets had been observed flying around her bedroom. At the same time the furniture began to move and the floors to creak. Lest you think that these were merely the delusions of an ageing crackpot, they were observed by members of the local constabulary. The police, bewildered by what they had seen, sealed the apartment and relocated Diakova to a new home. Nobody uttered the word 'poltergeist' at the time, and the weird goings-on were documented as an 'anomaly,' considered to be one of the first to be properly recorded in Europe. ❷ 22 Kreshchatyk.

The Bald Mountain of Vydubichi

Most bald peaks in folklore are thought to have been the result of pagans cutting down all the trees in that area to build a temple and in Christian times bald mountains frequently came to be considered places of evil. The Bald Mountain of Vydubichi has a long history that stretches back to the time of the warrior Batu-Khan. After capturing Kiev he ordered the death of all the residents. The Kyivians fled to the caves of Zverients and Kitayev. Enraged, Batu-Khan had the entrances to the caves bricked up. It is said that the restless souls of those who died still wander there. At the end of the 19th century a fort was built on the site and it was later used as a place of execution. All in all the Bald Mountain of Vydubichi has not been a happy place. ◉ Metro: Vydubichi or trolleybus 15 to the city limits.

The House with Chimeras

You won't have any trouble identifying this landmark, one of the weirdest buildings in the centre of the city. The facade and staircase at the front door are decorated with fantastic sculptures of chimeras and animals that seem to take their inspiration from the gargoyles of Paris's Notre Dame. Concrete-constructed heads of elephants, crocodiles, rhinoceros and antelope have been walled into this mysterious house. Elephants' trunks are used as gutters and sea monsters create part of the roof. The house was the creation of architect Vladislov Horodetsky, who considered hunting to be his true passion. Built as a present to himself for his 40th birthday, the house is one of the city's strangest buildings. ❷ 10 Bankova.

History

Kiev has long been an important commercial crossroads in Eastern Europe. The north-south trade route between the Vikings and Constantinople and the east-west trade route known as the Silk Road cross in Kiev, which made it important commercially and strategically, and so the victim of many invasions.

The legends say that the city, originally settled by Eastern Slavic tribes and referred to by many as the 'Mother of All Russian Cities', was founded sometime between AD480 and 560 by three brothers and one sister of the Polianian tribe. Sailing down the River Dnepr, the sister, Lybid, selected a spot to found a city. The city was named after the oldest brother, Kyi, while two of the hills in the area are named after the other brothers, Schek and Khoryv.

The Vikings were looking for an overland trade route from the north to Constantinople, and the route they chose took them through Kiev. By the middle of the 9th century, Viking princes had control of the city, and established a regime known as the Kievian Rus. In 860, Prince Oleh, from Russia, assassinated the ruling Viking princes and formed a vast empire running from the Baltic to Moldavia, with Kiev as its capital. Kiev would grow and prosper for nearly 400 years under the Kievian Rus. Written laws were established, and in 988 Orthodox Christianity was established as the official religion. In 1240, Mongols under Batu Khan (Genghis' grandson) captured and virtually destroyed the city. The Mongols did not stay around but Kiev did not recover and in 1362 the city was annexed to the Lithuanian principality. It started to grow again but in 1482 the Mongols invaded a second time and destroyed the city once again.

In 1569 Kiev (and most of Ukraine) came under Polish control. The Poles used fertile Ukraine as a breadbasket, as well as a buffer between them and the raiding hordes from the south and east. It was at this time that the country got its name, U-krayi-na, meaning 'borderland', or 'on the edge'. It was this period that saw the rise of the Cossacks and the possibility of an independent Ukrainian state. The Cossacks were local farmers who became great horsemen and warriors in order to defend their homes and farms against the attacking hordes. They grew in power and in 1654 drove the Poles out of Kiev, but were forced to form an alliance with Russia that brought them under Russian jurisdiction. Any hopes of Ukrainian independence were dashed in 1709, when Tsar Peter I won the battle of Poltava and took complete control of Ukraine but he made Kiev into a major centre and under 200 years of Tsarist rule the place grew and became a thriving, modern city.

During the Russian Revolution and civil wars from 1917 to 1921 Kiev changed hands 18 times as the Ukrainians fought unsuccessfully to free themselves from Russian Soviet rule. Both Lenin and Stalin wrought havoc on Ukraine, with famines, purges and genocide. More death and destruction fell on Kiev when the Nazis captured the city in June 1941. By the time the Russians recaptured the city in 1943 half of Kiev's population, including almost all of its Jewish community, had been killed. After the war, Russia started to rebuild the city. The Chernobyl disaster in 1986 triggered a push for independence and with the collapse of the Soviet Union Ukraine declared independence on 24 August 1991.

Since independence, Ukraine has suffered economic problems, mainly due to corruption, but Kiev has struggled through to start the reconstruction of its architectural and artistic masterpieces. The 'Orange Revolution' of November 2004 appears to have thrown out the last of the corrupt oligarchs from the Soviet era, and Kiev seems poised to become one of Europe's major capitals.

Lifestyle

Well into the second decade of Ukrainian independence, Kiev is striving hard to be the most prosperous and developed city in the country. An ever-evolving skyline is a testament to the improvements under way. But beneath the outward appearance of economic stability is the harsh reality of a still-poor country. Flashy, fashion-filled malls are surrounded by old women trying to make ends meet by selling vegetables or prized possessions. High-end Mercedes and SUVs with tinted windows careen past pedestrians waiting patiently for public transport. In Kiev these early days of the new republic are both the best of times and the worst of times.

The early years of independence were economically harsh for

most residents. Because so many people had either laboured in government factories, producing over-priced goods, or been members of the military, they saw their employment simply disappear with the creation of a new nation. Those who did remain employed often went several months without ever seeing a pay cheque. In addition, high inflation destroyed any pensions or savings that older people had. Despite the difficulties, they survived. This tenacious survival quality defines the Ukrainian personality.

If tenacity defines Ukrainian personality, then it is family that defines the Ukrainian soul. The family network goes way beyond the immediate family and incorporates parents, grandparents, aunts,

Looking your best is important, whether at a wedding or on a night out

uncles and cousins – dozens of cousins. Grandparents quite frequently are those who care for the children and in turn young adults care for the elderly. Ukrainians are very hospitable people and keen to engage in discussion with foreigners. Don't be surprised to be invited to their home, if only for a cup of tea (see the feature box).

No matter what economic conditions prevail, the residents of Kiev always manage to keep their urban style. Even if you can't afford the luxuries of life, there is still an appreciation of the finer things. Ukrainians always wear their best clothes and shoes in public, no matter how dire their circumstances. The Western impulse to dress casually when travelling is a difficult concept for most Kiev citizens to comprehend, so make an effort to dress nicely

🔺 *Relaxing with a drink is as much part of life in Kiev as in western cities*

and you'll find your reception more positive. After all, to Kyivians, if you are wealthy enough to travel to Kiev surely you must be able to dress well.

Cultural life is also strong in the city. Residents are well read and well versed in art, dance and music. Folk dancing remains popular at weddings and festivals. Handicrafts are an everyday part of life. As for music, Ukrainians sing when they are happy and sing when they are sad. Prepare to be fascinated by the merging of the new economy and independence with old traditions.

BEING A GOOD GUEST

- If you are invited to a family home, it is traditional to bring a gift. A bottle of wine, a cake or flowers are always appropriate. If there are children in the house, then it is considered good manners to bring a gift for them, too. If flowers are your choice of a gift make sure you bring an uneven number. Even numbers are reserved for funerals.
- Be ready to accept all food and drink that is presented to you. Refusing food is considered to be rude. Expect to receive a toast and be prepared to extend one in return. Make it flowery and long: simply saying 'cheers' just won't do.
- Be sure to remove your shoes when entering a home. Usually you will be given slippers to wear while inside.
- When visiting a church women should keep their heads covered, and men should remove their hats.
- If you are attending a business meeting, lunch or dinner, your dress should be conservative. Don't remove your suit jacket unless you are encouraged to do so.

Culture

Kiev is host to a wide range of cultural activities and venues. From classical opera and ballet to a Jackie Chan movie, the city has it all. And the very best part is that prices are cheaper than you would expect to pay in many other European cities – particularly if you are a student.

Kiev boasts a myriad places and palaces where you can enjoy a wide range of events from the National Opera or National Philharmonic for classical music to the Palace of Sport for rock and pop and the Ukraine Palace for Slavic music. Live theatre is also very popular and the city has nearly 20 active companies. Unfortunately almost all the productions are in the Ukrainian language. Better to stick with the ballet, where body language is almost universal.

The music and song of Ukraine are derived almost exclusively from the folk tradition of storytelling. Folk music comes from the epic poems known as *Bylyny* that told of the heroic deeds of courageous countrymen. These songs were carried across the country by wandering minstrels known as *kobzary*. It may seem like a good job to wander from town to town singing the glories of the nation, but a major drawback was that most minstrels were expected to be blind. To accompany their songs the *kobzary* used a lute-like instrument called a *kobza*. Eventually the *kobza* would be replaced by the *bandura*, a larger instrument that could have up to 65 strings! Today the *bandura* is regarded as the national instrument of Ukraine. You can hear performances of this music, and the chorus that accompanies the musicians, at the National Philharmonic and many other venues. A more sophisticated variety

---

◐ *Taras Shevchenko, the father of Ukrainian literature, is honoured all over Kiev*

of Ukrainian music has wedded the traditions of folk music to piano-based classical music. Composer Mykola Lysenko is credited with being the creator of this 'national music.'

If you have music it follows that you'll likely have dance. Ukrainian folk dancing for the most part is either Cossack or Hutsul. The Cossack dancers are known for their twirls, leaps and signature duck-kick. By contrast the Hutsul dancers perform more of a foot-stomping choreography. Either version will leave you breathless from simply watching the high-energy performances.

Arts and handcrafts comprise another important facet of cultural life in Ukraine. Kiev has certainly had its share of struggling artists and few have crossed into the Western art realm, possibly because classic romantic painting did not feature very strongly in Ukraine as it has in other parts of the world. The exceptions to this

● *The classical arts are alive and well at the National Opera and Ballet Theatre*

are Repin and Aivozovsky, whose works are displayed worldwide. The quintessential Ukrainian handcraft is the decoration of *pysanky* or Easter eggs. Using real eggs, wax and dyes, elaborate geometric designs cover the eggs. Flowers and animals are also popular egg decorations; the designs vary greatly from region to region. Other popular handcrafts are carved small wooden boxes, painted stove tiles and *rushniki*, embroidered hand-towels that are used for special occasions such as christenings, weddings, holiday meals and funerals.

With a literacy rate of 98 per cent, it shouldn't come as any surprise that literature plays an important part of the cultural life. Taras Shevchenko (see overleaf) is considered both a poet laureate and national hero. Other writers whose work has been translated for consumption in the West include Nikolay Vasilyevich Gogol (1809–52), who wrote *The Government Inspector*, *Dead Souls* and *Lesya Ukrayinka*. Ukrainians can also lay claim to works by Pushkin and Chekhov, who wrote and lived in the country for part of their lives. Owning books is somewhat of a status symbol and people are very possessive of their small personal libraries. A gift of a good book would always be welcome.

Not all culture in Kiev is classic or traditional. Pop culture is making serious inroads into the society. Pop music mixes folk tunes with modern beats, and the techno music you will hear has a distinct polka beat hiding under its modern cloak.

Even more popular than a night at the ballet or symphony is a night spent at the cinema. Going to a movie in Kiev requires that you not only buy a ticket, but book a seat. Pay a little more and opt for a chair in the upper deck, where you're less likely to have your sightline blocked. No language problem here: most new release films are shown in English.

TARAS SHEVCHENKO

You will not be in Kiev very long before you run into this name, and you will continue to run into it all over the city.

Shevchenko is a national hero in Ukraine, and is largely responsible for the Ukrainian language, culture and national image of today. A writer, mainly of poetry, he proved in many ways that the pen is mightier than the sword. Born in 1814 to a poor peasant family, he was orphaned as a young man but gained an education in St Petersburg and studied painting there. In 1840, he published his first poems. Many more publications followed.

An early revolutionary thinker, Shevchenko championed the causes of the poor peasants of Ukraine, Ukrainian independence and the Ukrainian language, which he used extensively in his writings. He referred to his homeland as 'this land of ours that is not our own'. Anti-Tsarist, he was banished to Siberia, which led to his early death in 1861.

Shevchenko's use of Ukrainian, rather than Russian, combined with his eloquence in it, elevated the language to a universally accepted form of expression in his native country. His writings, along with works of other Ukrainian writers, were banned in 1876, but the messages survived in the hearts of the Ukrainian people, helping give them an independent identity. His works are studied extensively in Ukrainian schools today and you will see reminders of him throughout Kiev and all of Ukraine.

● *More than one monument portrays the siblings who founded Kiev*

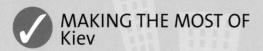

Shopping

When shopping in Kiev be prepared to have everyone, from the shop attendants to the street vendors, to only allow you to purchase what they deem is best for you. The attitude is definitely different from Western shopping, but this gentle interference is done with the best of intentions. The street vendor only wants you to have the freshest product, not necessarily the one you picked – so she will exchange it for you. The well-dressed shop women know their fashions and if something doesn't do you justice, they won't hesitate to let you know, or refuse to let you buy it! It is okay to be choosy; it shows good taste on your part. Just make sure you remember to be polite.

Shops in Kiev normally open at 10.00, close for lunch generally between 13.00 and 14.00, and then reopen until 20.00 in the evening. In just a few short years of independence, the city has been transformed from a place where it was difficult to buy anything to a place where you can buy almost everything.

If you want to shop with the rich and famous head for the underground Globus Shopping Complex at Maidan Nezalezhnosti. This is the largest of Kiev's shopping malls, with two floors laden with the glitz and glamour. Fashionistas also head to the Mandarin Plaza (ⓐ Baseina 4) for the most up-to-the-minute offerings.

Kiev is already beginning to show signs of globalised capitalism with mobile phone dealers, Nike and Reebok outlets. TsUM, the old Soviet-era department store at the intersection of Khreschatyk and Khmelnytskovo, is referred to by the locals as the Harrod's of Kiev. Even the once dingy underground passages of the metro are being

◗ *The quality of imported and local produce in the markets is high*

renovated as luxury and high-tech shops selling everything from perfume to laptop computers.

Are you ready to shop where the real people do? Head to one of the open markets such as Kontraktova Ploshca or Druzhby Narodiv, where you'll find piles of merchandise from Italy or Turkey. Be prepared to bargain.

If souvenirs are what you seek you'll find no lack of shops along Khreschatyk Street filled with *matroshkas* (what we call Russian dolls), *shapkas* (fur hats) and *narushniki* (embroidered towels). Some other traditional Ukrainian gifts are brightly painted woodenware, black,

BABUSHKAS

You will see many older women in traditional dark plain clothing and covered heads on the streets selling small items such as apples and shoelaces. Their plight is tragic, but their resolve is strong. As younger women, they were often left on their own for long periods of time as the menfolk were off doing military or other Soviet service. This made these women strong and independent. They were entitled to decent pensions under the old Soviet system; however, with independence, followed by massive inflation, their pensions, and what little savings they had, disappeared. Most are now penniless and depend on family members for food and shelter. Their strength and independent resolve drive them into the streets to do manual labour, or to sell small items on the street to make a little money to help out at home. Do not hesitate to buy from these women, and if you give them a little extra, you will get a smile that could melt an iceberg.

charcoal-fired pottery, and jewellery made from amber. The best souvenir market in the city is on Andriivsky uzviz. The street is always packed with tourists but be careful, not all you see is the real stuff.

You'll be disappointed if you hope to buy some authentic Soviet paraphernalia. It's mostly all gone. Today, anything with a red star emblazoned upon it has most likely been produced in China.

USEFUL SHOPPING PHRASES

What time do the shops open/close?
О котрій зачиняються відкриваються магазини?
O kotriy zachinyaietsya vidkrivayutjsa/mahaziny?

How much is this?
Скільки це коштує?
Skilki tse koshtuie?

What size is this?
Який це розмір?
Yakiy tse rozmir?

Can I try this on?
Я можу це приміряти?
Ya mozhu tse prymiryaty?

My size is...
Мій розмір ...
Miy rozmir...

I'll take this one, thank you
Я візьму це, спасибі
Ya viz'mu tse, spasybi

Can you show me the one in the window/this one?
Ви можете показати мені оце що на вітрині/оце?
Vy mozhete pokazaty meni otse scho na vitryni/otse?

Eating & drinking

LOCAL FARE

There are two staples to the Ukrainian diet, bread and *borscht*. Both come from the fertile lands that make up the country.

Ukraine has long been known as the breadbasket of Europe, and bread is central in the local culture. There is a traditional 'Bread and Salt' ceremony to welcome guests of honour, and the cry of 'Bread, Peace and Land' was used to rally the citizens during the Russian Revolution. The traditional bread is black, and made from rye flour and buckwheat. Visitors may not find it all that palatable, but other varieties, such as sourdough and white bread, are readily available. Bread is normally eaten with cheese, sausage or heavy cream.

Borscht, often mistakenly referred to as beetroot soup, starts with a vegetable or meat stock, to which is added cabbage, potatoes, and onions. Beetroot is added only to give colour and flavour. Other vegetables may be included, as are herbs such as dill. There is no set recipe, and the final product depends upon the cook and on what vegetables are available at the time of cooking. In many homes, especially among those of the not so well off, borscht is made in large quantities, and it may be served three times a day. If ordered in a restaurant, it will usually be served with bread and thick cream. Good borscht has a tangy flavour, and should be so thick that a spoon does not sink into it.

⊙ Borscht is more than a humble beetroot soup

Other local foods include dumplings stuffed with meat, cheese or potatoes. In season, the dumplings may be stuffed with fruit and as such make a good dessert. Another favourite is a mixture of rice and meat rolled up in cabbage leaves, and served with a tomato sauce. Meat is still considered luxury food in Ukraine, and when available, pork is preferred to beef. Fish and chicken are also popular. Chicken Kiev did originate here, but you will only find it on restaurant menus, not in private homes.

Ukrainians have a sweet tooth. Sweets, usually wrapped in bright-coloured paper, can be purchased from shops, street vendors and restaurants. The best sweets combine honey, nuts and chocolate. Ice cream is another favourite in Kiev, and it is eaten year round, even in the dead of winter.

RESTAURANTS

Kiev's restaurants are quickly becoming very cosmopolitan, so if you do not like, or have had enough of, the local cuisine, you will have no problem finding food from just about any other part of the world. Fast-food restaurants are growing in number, so it is easy to find burgers and pizza. Most of the better establishments have menus in

RESTAURANT CATEGORIES
The restaurant price guides used in the book indicate the approximate cost of a three-course meal for one person, excluding drinks, at the time of writing.
H Under 50Hr.   **HH** 50–100Hr.   **HHH** 100–150Hr.
HHH+ Over 150Hr.

● *Pavement cafés are plentiful in central Kiev*

English, and someone on the staff who speaks it. When ordering, make sure you understand the pricing structure of the restaurant you are in. In many cases, there are 'extras'. These can include bread and condiments. Also, some places charge by weight (usually per 100 grams), rather than portion, so be sure you know this before you 'super size' your order.

Breakfast does not seem to be in the Ukrainian lexicon, as Ukrainians tend to eat the same food for all three daily meals. Not to worry, most hotels serve a Western European-style buffet breakfast that includes breads, pastries, cereals, meats, cheeses and fresh fruit.

DRINKS

The national drink, if not the national pastime, in Ukraine is vodka. It is readily available in stores, and many families brew their own. The consumption of vodka is so high and so widespread that alcoholism is a major problem. Any excuse seems a good reason for a 'toast', and refusal of a drink when offered may be considered rude. Warning – do not try to match a Ukrainian drink for drink, and stick to known brand names. Homemade and bootleg vodka are common, and can give you stomach problems.

Other alcoholic beverages, such as beer and wine, are also readily available, but most of it is produced locally. You can find imported beer and wine at upmarket restaurants and shops.

Coffee and tea are served everywhere. However, adding milk or cream to either is unheard of here, so if you want white coffee or tea, you should plan to bring your own milk or cream. Fruit juices produced from locally grown fruit are common, but many are an acquired taste. Mineral water, both Ukrainian and imported, is easily obtained.

TIPPING

Tipping is not traditional in Ukraine, but is becoming more common, especially in Kiev. A tip of 10–15 per cent is recommended, especially in more upmarket restaurants and bars. Some restaurants are starting to add a 5–10 per cent service charge, so read the bill carefully when it arrives.

USEFUL DINING PHRASES

I would like a table for ... people.
Я хочу замовити столик на ... чоловік
Ya hochu zamovyty stolyk na ... cholovik

Excuse me, please may we order?
Вибачте, ми можемо зробити замовлення?
Vybachte, my mozhemor zrobyty zamovlennya?

Do you have any vegetarian dishes?
Чи є в Вас вегетаріанські страви?
Chi e v Vas vegetarians'ki stravi?

Where is the toilet (restroom) please?
Де знаходиться туалет?
De znahodytsya tualet?

May I have the bill, please?
Я можу отримати рахунок?
Ya mozhu otrymaty rahunok?

Entertainment & nightlife

Like most things in Kiev, the nightlife is a mix of the good, the bad and the weird. The city has an abundant mix of pubs and lounges, most of which are the haunts of foreigners and the local mafiosi. Because of the cost of alcohol, you'll quickly discover that most locals will buy a beer on the street and do their socialising outside when the weather permits. Wisely, the city closes the main street of Khreschatyk and the Podil district to vehicle traffic on weekends and holidays, so you'll only have to watch out for lurching pedestrians as opposed to a Lada driven by a drunk.

CLUBS, DISCOS & CASINOS

Just a touch of capitalism brings amazing changes to a night scene. Striptease is considered to be a 'classy' addition to a club, casinos operating 24 hours a day have sprung up like poppies and the most recent craze is *diskoteky*. The discos and dance clubs are a truly eclectic mix, as each new venue strives hard to outdo the other in lavishness and gimmickry – such as Dino, a dance club with a prehistoric theme, or the Tato Fashion Club, which parades models down a catwalk and then sends them out to dance with the

⬇ *Entertainment can be as simple as a mike and two guitars on the street*

patrons. And let's not leave the ladies behind! Kiev's first exotic dance club for women, Beverly Hills, has opened its doors. Women can enjoy the male form in many varieties. There's a menu that allows women to order a private dance, romantic dance, steamy shower or escort home with her favourite performer.

Care to gamble away the night? Kiev has plenty of places to lose your wages. Most of the casinos offer slots and traditional table games such as blackjack and roulette. You'll also find others that run raffles, poker games, and, of course, a strip show.

CLASSICAL & TRADITIONAL

Not all the nightlife will have you wishing you'd remained in your hotel room. Live theatre, opera, ballet, concerts, puppet shows and, yes, the circus are excellent ways to pass an evening in Kiev.

You may not understand the dialogue but there can be something magical about watching a play by Chekhov being performed in the country in which it was written. Part of the fun also comes from watching the other patrons, such as the families with young children, who come dressed up for the performance. Keep in mind that Kiev is a style-conscious city and it just won't do to dress down for a night on the town, no matter what the venue.

If the word ballet conjures up the phrase 'not my thing', think again. Governments may rise and fall, but the ballet in Kiev hasn't faltered a single step in maintaining its high quality. Seeing a ballet performed at this level of professionalism may well make you a ballet convert. Kiev's Opera is equally fascinating and there are performances almost every single night, and frequent matinées. To make it a truly local experience tr, the caviar and toast at intermission and don't forget to bring flowers for the ballerinas. (It's also okay to shout 'bravo' with gusto.) Classical music was once a fairly cheap outing in the city but prices have been on the increase and availability on the decrease. Performances of either classical or folk music occur almost every night.

Looking for something completely different? Try the Kiev Circus or the State Puppet Theatre. No need to worry about language difficulties with the circus – the glitz, the acrobatic feats and the animal acts speak their own language . Puppet performances are not just for children and there are several theatres that specialise in this type of entertainment. Puppets vary from the traditional marionettes to giant-size.

WHERE TO BUY TICKETS

Central Box Office @ Khreschatyk 21. ☎ 278 7642. 🌐 www.ctk.kiev.ua

Olvia @ Metrograd mall (from Rohnidynska str.) ☎ 247 5523. 🌐 www.olvia.com.ua 🕒 Daily 09.00–18.00.

🔺 *Kiev's National Opera House is as grand as that of any European capital*

Sport & relaxation

SPECTATOR SPORTS

The leading spectator sport in Kiev is football, and Dynamo Kiev is a world-famous and very successful football team. Ukrainian football player Andriy Shevchenko is a national hero who was recently named European Footballer of the Year. Dynamo Stadium, very close to the city centre, is the home of Dynamo Kiev, although few of the team's matches are played there. Kick-off is around 19.00; tickets cost 2–10Hr. and can be purchased from ticket windows and pre-match tables near the stadium entrance.

Olympic (Respublikansky) Stadium is where most of Dynamo Kiev's European matches are played. It was built in 1980 as one of the Olympic sites. The reason is fairly obvious – it holds 100,000 people as opposed to Dynamo Stadium's 15,000. Kick-off is around

● *Hidropark is Kiev's main centre for outdoor activities*

17.00, and tickets are 2–10Hr., purchased from ticket windows at the stadium.

Dynamo Stadium ⓐ Hrushevskoho 3. ⓣ 229 0209. Ⓜ Metro: Maidan Nezalezhnosti.

Olympic (Respublikansky) Stadium ⓐ Chervonoarmiiyska 55. ⓣ 246 7007. Ⓜ Metro: Respublikansky Stadion.

Boxing has become another popular spectator sport, especially since two Ukrainian brothers, Vitaliy (Doctor Ironfist) and Volodomyr Klychko have achieved international prominence.

Winter sports such as ice hockey, skiing and ice skating are very popular. Ukraine has produced many Olympic Champions, especially in hockey and figure skating.

ACTIVITIES

Summer activities centre around the River Dnepr. Boating is a favourite, as Kyivians take to the waters of the Dnepr to cool down from the summer heat. Boat rides of 1–2 hours are available at the boat terminal at Poshtova ploscha in Podil.

Hidropark, accessed by the metro station of the same name, is a recreation area built on two islands in the middle of the river. It features sandy beaches, and trails through forests and marshes. Swimming in the river is not recommended, because of pollution. However, there are two swimming pools on site. Amusement rides, a volleyball court, a night club and food vendors can also be found there.

Hidropark Ⓜ Metro: Hidropark.

Ice fishing is a curious winter activity. Fishermen chop a hole in the ice on the river, and drop in a baited line. They also normally consume large quantities of vodka, used as anti-freeze against the cold blowing winds on the river.

Accommodation

Kiev has many hotels and other accommodation. The price and quality run the full gamut from outstanding and expensive to cheap and dirty, unfortunately sometimes both in the same hotel. The standard three- or four-star rating system does not work well in Kiev, as hotels with wonderful lobbies and restaurants can have miserable rooms upstairs. Pricing is not always a good indicator of quality either, as price seems to depend on what they think they can get, rather than on what they are going to give you.

Timid travellers may want to stick to the hotels of well established international chains. The more adventurous may want to try something local. In any case, be sure to see your room, and have a settled price, before signing in.

PRICE RATING
All are approximate prices for a single night in a double room/two persons; breakfast is often included.
H Under 300Hr. **HH** 300–600Hr. **HHH** 600–1000 Hr.
HHH+ Over 1000Hr.

HOTELS
Holosiyivsky H Located in the south part of the city. Rooms are cheap, but you get what you pay for. ❸ 50-richchia Zhovtnia 93. ❶ 258 2911. ⓦ www.hotelgolos.kiev.ua

Central Railway Station H Kiev's main station has overnight rooms available for those arriving late or departing early. The rooms are nice, but bathrooms are shared. ❸ Vokzalna pl. 2. ❶ 223 1111.

Druzhba HH In the southern part of town, close to the Lybidska metro station. ⓐ Druzhby Narodiv bulvar. 5. ⓣ 528 3406.

Express HH This hotel is near the main railway station, and contains the central booking office for the railway system. Recently renovated, the interior is quite nice, although the exterior is rather stark. ⓐ Tarasa Shevchenka bulvar 38–40. ⓣ 239 8995. ⓦ www.expresskiev.com.ua

Kozatsky HH Located in the centre of the city, overlooking the Maidan Nezalezhnosti. ⓐ Mykhailivska 1–3. ⓣ 279 4925. ⓦ www.kozatsky.kiev.ua

Myr HH In the south of the city, very near the Central Bus Station, this is a Soviet-style high-rise. Most of it has recently been remodelled, but the rooms can be small. ⓐ Holosiivskyi prospekt. 70. ⓣ 264 9646. ⓦ www.hotelmir.kiev.ua

Prolisok HH On the western approach to the city, convenient to those driving in, this is designed more as a motel, and features attractive rooms and cottages. ⓐ Peremohy prospekt 139. ⓣ 451 8038. ⓦ www.prolisok.com.ua

Sport HH This is another Russian-style high-rise, located south of the centre of the city. It is close to the Respublikansky Stadion metro station, and has a casino. ⓐ Chervonoarmiyska 55A. ⓣ 220 0252. ⓦ www.h-sport.kiev.ua

Turist HH Kiev's largest hotel complex looks like a Russian apartment block on the outside. It is nicer inside. Located on the left bank, it is close to the Livoberezhna metro station, the river and Hidropark. It features restaurants, internet access, a bar and a tourist bureau. If you do not mind riding the metro into town, the rooms are good value. ❷ Raisy Okipnoy 2. ❶ 568 4254. ❿ www.hotel-tourist.kiev.ua

Ukraina HH The convenient location near Maidan Nezalezhnosti is about all this hotel has going for it. The rooms are tolerable, but the staff are reputed to be rude. ❷ Instytutska 4. ❶ 228 2804. ❿ www.ukraine-hotel.kiev.ua

Adria HHH This is part of the Turist Hotel complex, but far more luxurious. The complex features restaurants, internet access, a bar and a tourist bureau. ❷ Raisy Okipnoy 2. ❶ 516 2457. ❿ www.adria.kiev.ua

Boatel Dniprovsky HHH A unique hotel floating on the River Dnepr in the Podil area of the city, with a restaurant. ❷ Naberezhno-Khreschatytska 10A, moorage 2. ❶ 490 9055. ❿ www.capitan-club.kiev.ua

Domus HHH In the centre of Podil, and a favourite of businessmen. Recently renovated, it features an Italian restaurant. ❷ Yaroslavska 19. ❶ 462 5120. ❿ www.domus-hotel.kiev.ua

Hotel Gintama HHH A smaller, friendly, family-run hotel, this place is near St Alexander's Catholic Church in the centre of the city. ❷ Trokhsviatytelska 9. ❶ 278 5092. ❿ www.gintama.com.ua

Khreschatyk HHH Located in the centre of town and with comfortable rooms, the Khreschatyk features a bar, two restaurants

and a sauna, as well as airline offices for LOT, Lufthansa, CSA, Air France and Finnair. ❸ Khreschatyk 14. ❶ 279 7339.
Ⓦ www.khreshatik.kiev.ua

Kiev HHH The Kiev, in the historic district just south of the city centre, close to the Ukrainian Parliament, features a bar, restaurant, banquet halls and shops. ❸ M. Hrushevskoho 26/1. ❶ 253 0155.
Ⓦ www.hotelkiev.com.ua

Lybid HHH Conveniently near the main railway station, and built in 1970, the Lybid has three restaurants, a bar, a dance floor, an American sports bar and a sporting goods store. ❸ Peremohy prospekt 1. ❶ 236 0063. Ⓦ www.hotellybid.com.ua

President-Hotel Kievsky HHH One of the most comfortable hotels in Kiev, built in 1980, it boasts a convention centre, a fitness centre with pool, a casino, three bars, a café, a hairdresser, a sauna and excellent concierge services. It is located near the Olympic Stadium in central Kiev. ❸ Hospytalna 12. ❶ 289 4144. Ⓦ www.ukrhotel.com

Rus HHH Rus is a leading hotel in Kiev and is lavishly decorated with mosaics and sculptures. Built in 1979, it contains a convention centre, two restaurants, three bars and two banqueting halls, but the rooms are reasonable priced. It is located near the Olympic Stadium in the city centre. Avis Car Rental is on site. ❸ Hospytalna 4. ❶ 256 4000.
Ⓦ www.hotelrus.kiev.ua

Salyut HHH A hotel with a unique cylindrical shape, Salyut is located very near the Caves Monastery, and has a casino. ❸ Sichnevoho Povstannia 11A. ❶ 251 1199. Ⓦ www.salutehotel.kiev.ua

Vozdvyzhensky HHH This small hotel is near the city centre, close to Andrew's descent, but its location away from the busy streets ensures that its rooms are quiet. It has recently been refurbished to cater to Western tastes.
ⓐ Vozdvyzhenska 60. ① 531 9900. Ⓦ www.vozdvyzhensky.com

Dnepr HHH+ A luxury hotel in the centre of Kiev, this is a leftover from the Soviet era; in fact only the suites and larger rooms are luxurious, the standard rooms being rather small. It does, however, have an outstanding restaurant. ⓐ Khreschatyk 1–2. ① 254 6777. Ⓦ www.dniprohotel.kiev.ua

Impressa HHH+ Luxurious and very clean, this small hotel in the centre of the Podil area features a casino on site. ⓐ Sahaidachnoho 21. ① 239 2939. Ⓦ www.impressa.com.ua

Natsionalny HHH+ Located just south of the city centre near the Parliament, and frequented by government officials. The rooms, if you can get one, are very good. ⓐ Lypska 5. ① 255 8888. Ⓦ www.natsionalny.kiev.ua

Premier Palace HHH+ This is considered by some to be Kiev's best and most impressive hotel. Located in the centre of the city, it offers a health club, a business centre and excellent service. The 8th-floor restaurant gives a panoramic view of the city. ⓐ Tarasa Shevchenka bulvar 5–7. ① 244 1200. Ⓦ www.premier-palace.com

Radisson SAS HHH+ Opened in 2005, the first international chain hotel in Kiev, the Radisson SAS is expected to raise the benchmark when it comes to standards of hotel service in the city. It is located

just west of the city centre. @ Yaroslaviv Val 22–24. ☏ 492 2200.
Ⓦ www.radissonsas.com

HOSTELS

Kiev International Youth Hostel H About 15 minutes from the centre
of Kiev by metro, this hostel has an English-speaking reception open
09.00–21.00. @ Artema 52A. Ⓦ www.hostelworld.com

Yaroslav International Youth Hostel H Handily located in the historic
Podil area, this hostel has English-speaking staff and a 24-hour
reception. @ Yaroslavska 10. Ⓦ www.hostelworld.com

The distinctive Hotel Salyut isn't difficult to spot

THE BEST OF KIEV

There are a lot of new sights and experiences waiting for you in Kiev and the surrounding countryside, easily enough to fill a week – or longer, if you plan on making an expedition to Lviv (Lvov) or Odessa to get yet another picture of Ukrainian life.

TOP 10 ATTRACTIONS

Here is our selection of ten sights and experiences that should be top of your list on a visit to Kiev.

- **The Caves Monastery** The most popular attraction in Kiev. If you see nothing else, you must visit this (page 90).

- **Maidan Nezalezhnosti (Independence Square) & Khreschatyk Street** This is where it 'happens' in Kiev (see page 70).

- **Andriivsky uzviz (Andrew's Descent)** A lot to see and do on this street, whether it's visiting St Andrew's Church or buying all your souvenirs here (see page 73).

- **Podil** There is much to see, do and eat in this small corner of Kiev (see page 100).

- **Cathedrals** St Sophia's is Kiev's most beautiful church (see page 75). St Vladimir's is where you should go to join the Kyivians for an Orthodox service, a truly moving experience (see page 74).

- **The Shevchenko National Opera and Ballet Theatre** A trip to Kiev is not complete without an evening spent here. Even if you think you don't like ballet, a performance by the Kiev Ballet may change your mind (see page 78).

- **Babi Yar** No one can fail to be affected by this memorial to the victims of Nazi genocide (see page 108).

- **The National History Museum & the Desiatynna Church Ruins** The best place to get a feel for the country's history (see page 76).

- **The Pyrohovo Museum of Folk Architecture and Life** Get a good look at how the people lived on the Ukrainian land in centuries past (see page 110).

- **Chernobyl** The site of the nuclear disaster is a must-see destination for many, however macabre (see page 112).

▼ *The complex of buildings around St Sophia's is one of Kiev's top sights*

This is a quick guide to getting the most from a short visit to Kiev, depending on the amount of time you have available.

HALF-DAY: KIEV IN A HURRY

If you only have half a day, especially the morning half, try to get to the Caves Monastery. Go as early as possible, and go to the Lower Lavra. If you have time after visiting the caves, then start to explore the Upper Lavra.

If the caves are not your thing, and you want to see part of the city, then the following walk will take you round many of the best central sights. Start by walking round Maidan Nezalezhnosti (Independence Square), with its statues, monuments and fountains and then head south down the east side of Khreschatyk Street. Look out for the big TsUM store across the street at the intersection of Bodana Khmelnytskoho. Where Khreschatyk intersects with Tarasa Shevchenka, you will find the Bessarabsky market. Cross under the street to Tarasa Shevchenka and continue west.

A short side trip south on Volodomyrska will take you to Kiev University. At the intersection of Ivana Franka, you will find the Fomin Botanical Gardens on your left and St Vladimir's Cathedral on your right. From here it's a short walk to the Shevchenko Opera and Ballet Theatre. Continue north on Volodomyrska, and you will pass the Golden Gate and St Sophia's Cathedral. At Sophia's Square, stay on Volodomyrska until you reach Desiatynna, where you will find the Desiatynna ruins and St Andrew's Church.

At the end of a frenetic morning, find an outdoor café, sit down and have a nice cold Ukrainian beer and a bowl of borscht!

1 DAY: TIME TO SEE A LITTLE MORE

Start early in the morning to avoid the crowds, and head for the

Caves Monastery. Start with the Lower Lavra and the caves themselves, then explore the Upper Lavra. Return to Maidan Nezalezhnosti (Independence Square) for a light lunch, and then take the half-day walking tour already suggested. Depending on time and stamina, you may take a side trip down Andrew's Descent into Kontraktova Square in Podil. Explore the square, then continue east on Sahaidachnoho and take the funicular up to St. Michael's Monastery.

Finish the day with a leisurely meal at one of the riverfront restaurants in Podil.

2–3 DAYS: SHORT CITY-BREAK

After you have done the one-day activities, take some time to go back to explore the museums and churches that interest you, to walk around Podil, shop for souvenirs on Andrew's Descent, and to attend a performance of the opera or ballet. Other experiences would be a trip to Babi Yar, attending an Orthodox church service, strolling through the Botanical Gardens, or joining the shopping melee in Bessarabsky market or Kontraktova Ploscha. Pick up some bread, cheese and wine at one of the many supermarkets, and go to Hydropark to enjoy a picnic lunch on the banks of the river. In the evening, try one of the many nightclubs, or try your luck at one of the many casinos in the city.

LONGER: ENJOYING KIEV TO THE FULL

If you have longer, and you have seen all you want to see in Kiev, then plan a day trip to Chernobyl, or to the Pyrohovo Museum of Folk Architecture and Life. For a complete contrast take an overnight train ride to Lviv, another beautiful but quite different Ukrainian city, well worth visiting for a few days.

Something for nothing

One advantage of visiting Kiev is that many of the sights and attractions are free, or have a very small admission fee.

Kiev is a city of churches, many of which have recently been renovated, and, as they are still owned by the church, are open to the public. There is no entrance fee to these churches, although visitors are expected to purchase a candle, which cost from 1–3Hr. Other churches have been converted to museums and although there is an entrance fee it is usually quite low, 5Hr. or less.

The main attraction in Kiev is the Caves Monastery. Although there is an entrance fee to the monastery complex, entrance to the caves themselves is free. You can even avoid paying the entry fee: simply travel about 300 m south of the main entrance on Sichnevoho Povstannia and enter via the Lower Lavra entrance.

Central Kiev and Podil are fairly compact, making them quite walkable. It costs nothing to walk the streets to view the buildings, monuments, and statues and to enjoy the many parks. It is possible to get a feel for the city and its culture without having to pay anything.

FREE ATTRACTIONS
- Babi Yar (see page 108)
- Caves of the Lower Lavra (see page 90)
- CCA (The Soros Center of Contemporary Art) (see page 103)
- Desiatynna (Tithing) Church ruins (see page 74)
- Mykhaylivska Zolotoverkhyi Monasterya (St Michael's Golden-Domed Monastery) (see page 75)
- Pokrovska Convent with St Nikolai's Cathedral (see page 110)
- St Vladimir's Cathedral (see page 74
- Vydubytsky Monastery (see page 97)

ATTRACTIONS FOR 5HR. OR LESS

- Chernobyl National Museum (see page 100)
- Museum of One Street (see page 103)
- Museum of the Great Patriotic War (see page 97)
- National History Museum (see page 76)
- St Andrew's Church (see page 74)
- St Sophia's Cathedral (the grounds, but not the church itself) (see page 75)

⬇ *Vydubytsky is just one of Kiev's many monasteries that are free to enter*

When it rains

No need to despair for lack of things to do in Kiev when the weather turns dismal. You'll discover a wealth of activities and experiences inside many of the city's great treasures.

If it rains (or snows) on a Sunday, or any other day, go to church. St Vladimir's Cathedral is one of the most artistic churches in the city. Built in the Byzantine style, it has a bright yellow exterior capped with seven black domes. Inside, the walls are covered with paintings depicting the spiritual history of the city. You can combine the beauty of an Orthodox service with your sightseeing. St Vladimir's is a favourite church for Kyivians, making this a truly authentic experience. Services are held daily at 08.00 and 17.00 and on Sunday at 0.700, 10.00 and 17.00.

Inclement days are perfect for the interiors of museums. The National History Museum provides an excellent overview of the Ukrainian history from prehistoric times to the present. The collections are wide and varied including books, art, artefacts, archaeological finds and even coins.

If it must be art and art alone for your dreary day, head to the National Art Museum. The collection inside is largely unknown to the Western world and you'll be in for a few surprises. Most of the works, not surprisingly, are by Ukrainian artists and span a time period from the 14th to the 20th centuries.

Meteorological conditions can even force you underground! Or is that just another excuse to go shopping? Globus is a lively underground mall featuring lots of recognisable Western labels such as Polo and Esprit. The stores open and close with the metro station timetable so you can spend as long as you or your wallet hold out. Metrograd is another underground mall worthy of exploration: in general the prices and quality are lower than those at Globus. For a truly posh experience head for the Manadarin Plaza. This is where the Kyivian upper crust comes to shop for designer fashions from around the world.

And, of course, there are always movies, plays, puppet shows, concerts and operas to keep you both amused and dry.

When the weather's bad, head underground for some retail therapy

On arrival

TIME DIFFERENCES

Kiev, like the rest of Ukraine, is on Eastern European Time (EET), GMT+2 hours in winter. It changes to Daylight Saving time (GMT+3 hours) from the first Sunday in April to the last Sunday in October. In Ukrainian summer time, when it is 12.00 noon in Kiev, the time at home is as follows:

Australia Eastern Standard Time 19.00, Central Standard Time 18.30, Western Standard Time 17.00
New Zealand 21.00
South Africa 11.00
UK and Republic of Ireland 10.00
USA and Canada Newfoundland Time 06.30, Atlantic Canada Time 06.00, Eastern Time 05.00, Central Time 04.00, Mountain Time 03.00, Pacific Time 02.00, Alaska 01.00.

ARRIVING

By air

Most international flights arrive at Kiev Boryspol State International Airport, which is 35 km (22 miles) east of the city. You can expect to take up to an hour to clear customs and immigration, although recent changes in visa requirements should speed this up (see page 140). The airport is small, but modern. It has currency exchanges, ATMs, duty-free, a post office and telephones. There is also a bar that has internet access. You should obtain some local currency on arrival, as Ukraine is still largely a cash economy, and taxis and shops may not take euros, dollars or credit cards.

To get into Kiev you can take an Atass bus in front of the

International Terminal. The trip takes up to an hour, and costs 10Hr. The bus takes you to the new south terminal of the Kiev central railway station. Buses leave every 15–30 minutes, 05.00–01.00. You can also take a taxi to the centre of town. The cost is about 100Hr., and takes 30–45 minutes.

Boryspil Airport ☎ 296 7609 or 296 7243.

ⓦ www.airport-borispol.kiev.ua

Atass Bus ☎ 296 7367.

Kiev is rightly proud of its recently modernised Voksal (railway station)

By rail

The central railway station has recently been refurbished and expanded, with a new, ultra-modern south terminal. It is one of the best in Europe, and uses English signs and listings as well as Cyrillic. There are currency exchanges, ATMs and public phones. The station has overnight rooms to rent (see page 44) for those arriving late or departing early. The rooms are inexpensive, but clean and secure, although the bathrooms are down the hall.

The station is close to the centre of town. Although you can walk, you may want to take a taxi, metro (Vokzal'na station), trolleybus, bus or minivan. Taxis tend to overcharge people picked up at the railway station.

Central railway station ⊜ Vokzal'na pl. 1. ☎ 465 2111.

By bus

All international and national buses stop at the central bus station, although many incoming buses will stop at other bus terminals that may be closer to your destination in Kiev. The central bus station is badly in need of renovation, so do not plan to spend any time there. There are a currency exchange, an ATM, a café and public phones. The central bus station is in the south part of the city. You can take a taxi or a trolleybus into the city centre and the Lybidska metro station is nearby.

Central bus station ⊜ Moskovs'ka pl. 3. ☎ 265 5774.

Driving

Driving to Kiev is only for the brave. Highway E-40 runs from Western Europe directly into Kiev. Driving in the city can be difficult, as street signs are in Cyrillic, and posted on buildings in positions that are often hard to see. Although the streets are in generally good condition, there is no logic to their layout, and they are often closed for celebrations. You will find some rather rough tram track crossings. Construction zones are poorly marked, and can prove dangerous, especially at night. Parking is also a problem in Kiev. There are state-owned parking lots around the city, and you should only park in designated spots, and in areas that are well lit and secure.

FINDING YOUR FEET

Few people in Kiev speak English, and most signs are in Cyrillic, so you will want to stay in the city centre and Podil, which are the major tourist areas, and areas where most English is spoken. As you get further from the city centre, the underlying poverty becomes more obvious, fewer and fewer people speak English, and facilities that can help or cater for visitors become fewer and fewer.

IF YOU GET LOST, TRY ...

Excuse me. Do you speak English?
Перепрошую. Ви розмовляєте по-англійськи?
Pareproshuiu. Vy rozmovlyaite po-anglyis'ky?

Excuse me, is this the right way to...?
Вибачте, я правильно йду до ...?
Vybachte, ya pravyl'no yidu do...?

Can you point to it on my map?
Ви можете показати, де це на карті?
Vy mozhete pokazaty, de tse na karti?

Babi Yar

Pokrovska Convent

Peremohy pros

Tarasa Shevchn

Borschahivska vul.

Kosmonavta Komarova pros.

Centr.
Railw
Statio

Che

0   1km

N

ORIENTATION

Maidan Nezalezhnosti, or Independence Square, is the centre of the city, and the meeting place in Kiev. It is a good place to start any exploration of the city. Many bus and tram routes converge here, as do two of the metro lines. Maidan Nezalezhnosti lies on Khreschatyk Street, a wide street that runs south-west past the square towards the Olympic Stadium. Directly west of Maidan Nezalezhnosti are the parks that line the River Dnepr, and then the river itself, Hydropark and the left bank.

About 1 km (²/₃ mile) due north of Maidan Nezalezhnosti are the funicular and stairways that take you down into Podil and the banks of the River Dnepr. Due south of Maidan Nezalezhnosti is the historic area of Pechersk, with the parliament buildings and the Caves Monastery.

GETTING AROUND

Kiev is a very large city, but fortunately, most of the sights and attractions are within 2 km (1 ¼ mile) of Maidan Nezalezhnosti, and many within half that distance, and so walking is feasible for most sightseeing.

If you want to wander further than your feet can take you, Kiev has an excellent public transport system. The metro (subway) has three lines, and is fast, clean, reliable and safe, not to mention inexpensive. One ride costs only 50 kopecks, but you need to purchase tokens which are available at the station entrances. Signs are in Cyrillic, so be sure you know where you are going before you start. Most of the metro system is deep underground, so expect a long escalator ride to get from the street to the stations.

Buses, trolleybuses and trams can also get you around, but they

---

● *The metro is a safe, clean and speedy way to reach Kiev's outlying sights*

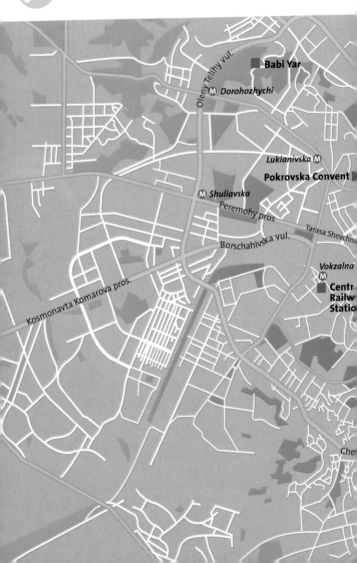

Babi Yar

Ⓜ *Dorohozhychi*

Oleny Telihy vul.

Lukianivska Ⓜ

Pokrovska Convent

Ⓜ *Shuliavska*

Peremohy pros

Tarasa Shevchn

Borschahivska vul.

Vokzalna
Ⓜ
**Centr
Railw
Statio**

Kosmonavta Komarova pros.

Che

rasa Shevchenka

Naberezhno - Khreschatyska vul.

PODIL M

raktova Pl. M

Poshtova Pl. M

DNIPROVSK

Maidan
Nezalezhnosti M

Livoberezhna M

Teatralna M

Dynamo Kiev Stadium

versitets M

Khreschatyk M

BESSARABSKA

Arsenalna M

Naberezhne Shose

Brovarsky pros.

Hidropark M

Hidropark

Pl. Tolstoho M

Palars Sportu M

Klovska M

Dnipro M

River Dnepr

publikansky M

PECHERSK

Vozziednannia pros.

Palars Ukraina M

Pecherska M

KATAJANOKKA

Druzhby
Narodiv M

Druzhby Narosliv bulv.

Lybidska M

yi pros.

Bus Station

Saperno Slobidska vul.

Vydubichi M

N

0   1km

Mykoly Bazhana pros.

are slow because of the heavy traffic and they tend to be very crowded, so use them only for short hops. Tickets are 40–60 kopecks, and can be purchased from drivers and conductors.

Marshrutka are a cross between a bus and a taxi. They are minibuses, usually Mercedes vans that use regular bus stops. They are much quicker than buses and trams, but cost much more, from 1 to 3Hr. They can also be very crowded.

Taxis are everywhere, although few are metered. Every horror story you have heard about taxi drivers applies in Kiev. They drive like crazy and they will try to overcharge you. Settle on a price to your destination before you climb into the taxi, then hang on and pray. The best place to sit in a taxi is directly behind the driver, as he is less likely to hit something on his side of the car. It is normally cheaper to flag a taxi than to phone for one. Two of the more reliable taxi companies are:

Kiev-Taxi ☎ 459 0101.

Taxi-Blue ☎ 296 4243.

CAR HIRE

Driving in Kiev is considered foolhardy at best, so do not even think about it unless you have no other choice. Daily rates are very high, as is insurance. It is wiser to stick with the big international rental agencies, and be sure to have lots of insurance, as car thieves favour rental cars. Most car rental agencies offer chauffeur services, which may be worth the extra cost if you just want to sightsee by car.

Avis ⓐ Hospytalna 4 (Hotel Rus). ☎ 490 7333. Ⓦ www.avis.com.ua

Europcar ⓐ Horkoho 48A. ☎ 238 2691. Ⓦ www.europcar.ua

Hertz Rent A Car ⓐ Pymonenka 13. ☎ 494 4935.
Ⓦ www.hertz.com.ua

▶ *Kiev is a city of golden domes – these are at the Monastery of the Caves*

Central Kiev

This is a relatively small section near the geographical centre of the city. It is the pulsing heart of Kiev, where most of the political, business and tourist action happens. It is bounded on the east by the River Dnepr, on the north by Podil (see page 100), on the south by the monastery area of Pechersk (see page 90), and on the west by the central railway station.

SIGHTS & ATTRACTIONS

Maidan Nezalezhnosti (Independence Square)

This urban space has become the focal point of Kiev, much like Piccadilly Circus in London, or Times Square in New York. It gained international prominence at the end of 2004 during the 'Orange Revolution' when it filled with citizens protesting at an improper election.

The square is filled with fountains and statues, including a bronze sculpture of the four legendary siblings who founded Kiev – Kyi, Lybid, Shchek and Khoriv (see page 16). A newer addition is the Independence Monument, erected in 2001. Above ground, the square is active with food and souvenir stands, where in the evening people congregate to enjoy a drink while listening to street musicians; below ground is a large shopping centre.

Khreschatyk vulitsia

Running south from Independence Square, this is Kiev's main north–south artery. One of the oldest streets in Kiev, it is just under 2 km (just over 1 mile) long. The buildings lining the street were completely destroyed in World War II but Khreschatyk is now lined

with shops, boutiques and restaurants. During weekends, Khreschatyk becomes pedestrian-only, and the local populace comes out to party.

Verkhovna Rada (National Parliament)

This building and the Marinsky Palace form one site. The members of the Ukrainian parliament meet beneath its glass dome, and it was here on 24 August 1991 that Ukrainian independence was declared. The building is not open to visitors.

Marinsky Palace

The palace was built in 1755 as a residence for royalty visiting Kiev

Even though you can't go inside, the Marinsky Palace is well worth a visit

and is named after Maria, wife of Tsar Alexander II. The beautiful blue and cream coloured building was designed by Italian architect Bartholomeo Rastrelli in a Russian baroque style, similar to that of the summer palace in St Petersburg. The building is closed to the public and used mainly for special occasions by the Ukrainian President. However, the grounds are beautiful, and it is worth a walk around.

② Hrushevskoho 5.

Andriivsky uzviz (Andrew's Descent)
Named after the Apostle (see box overleaf), this quaint cobblestoned street winds its way downhill from the city centre to Podil. Near the top it is packed with souvenir and local handicraft

> ### THE LEGEND OF ST ANDREW
> Andriivsky uzviz (Andrew's Descent) is named after St Andrew, the first disciple of Christ. A local legend has it that the Apostle sailed up the River Dnepr, landed near here, climbed the hill and planted a cross. St Andrew is also said to have predicted the formation of a great city on the site.

stalls that will sell you anything from the traditional 'Russian' dolls to weird T-shirts. Towards the bottom, you will find local artists displaying their work and several good art galleries. Along the way you may see musicians, mime artists and poets, all looking for a hand-out. There are food vendors, but few places to sit down to eat. At the top of the Descent is **St Andrei's (Andrew's) Church**, which was completed in 1762 by Rastrelli, the architect of the Marinsky Palace. The beautiful and colourful baroque church is now a museum. Across the street from St Andrew's are the remains of the **Desiatynna (Tithing) Church**. Originally built in 989 as the Mother of God Church, it was destroyed during the Mongol invasion of 1240.

St Vladimir's Cathedral
This is one of Kiev's newer churches, started in 1862 and completed in 1892. It is probably the most highly decorated church in the city, and its grand opening was attended by Tsar Nicholas II. It was built in Byzantine style, with a bright yellow exterior and seven black domes. The artwork inside is awesome, with large painting on the walls and ceilings depicting the spiritual history of Kiev. This is the church still much used by the people of Kiev, so if you want to see an Orthodox service, this is the place.

ⓐ Tarasa Shevchenka 20. ① 235 0362. ⓛ Services daily 08.00 and 17.00, Sun 07.00, 10.00 and 17.00. Ⓜ Metro: Universitet.

Sofiysky Sobor (St Sophia's Cathedral)

Kiev's oldest standing church was completed in 1031. Inside are mosaics and other artwork dating back to the time of construction. The church's Byzantine architecture derives from that of Constantinople (Istanbul), capital of the Eastern Orthodox Church at the time. The most important mosaic is the Virgin Orans, which has great significance to the Orthodox religion, and is now on the UNESCO World Heritage List of protected sites. In front of the cathedral is a statue of Bohdan Khmelnytsky, the Cossack hero who liberated Kiev from the Poles, only to cede control of it to the Russians. ⓐ Volodomyrska 24. ① 278 2083. Ⓦ www.sophia.org.ua ⓛ Thur–Tues 10.00–17.30.

Mykhaylivska Zolotoverkhyi Monasterya (St Michael's Golden-Domed Monastery)

Named after Kiev's patron saint, this is the home of the Kiev Patriarch of the Ukrainian Orthodox Church. The original was built in 1108 but was destroyed by the Russians in 1936. After independence it was rebuilt and opened in 2001. It features medieval/baroque styling with seven bright gold domes. There is a monastery museum on site. On the square surrounding the monastery is a monument to the 5 million victims of the great famines of 1932 and 1933. Also on the square are statues of St Andrew, Princess Olga and the Byzantine Sts Cyril and Methodius, who invented the Cyrillic alphabet and brought literacy to the Slav peoples.
ⓐ Mykhailivska ploscha. ① 228 6268.

The House with Chimeras

The strangest building in Kiev, decorated with gargoyles and other weird animals, it was built around 1900 by architect Vladislov Horodetsky (for more details, see page 15). Today it houses presidential administration offices.

📍 Bankova 10.

Zoloti Vorota (Golden Gate)

This is a replica of the main entrance to Kiev and the surrounding ramparts, erected in 1037, which protected Kiev before destruction in the Mongol invasion of 1240. The reconstruction was completed in 1982 and is currently undergoing renovation. A monument to Yaroslav the Great, a Ukrainian hero who successfully defended Kiev against raiding tribes called Pechenegs, stands in front of the gate.

📍 Volodomyrska at Yaroslaviv. Ⓜ Metro: Zoloti Vorota.

Lenin Statue

Yes, there is one remaining statue of Lenin in Kiev. It probably escaped because it is rather modest. Get a picture while you can, as it may not last.

📍 Bessarabaska ploscha, at the eastern end of Tarasa Shevchenka.

CULTURE

National History Museum

The museum covers Ukrainian history from prehistoric times up to the present. The collections are extensive, including art, archaeological artefacts, old books and coins. The museum is located

---

▶ *Zoloti Vorota is a reconstruction of one of the legendary Great Gates of Kiev*

near St Andrew's Church and the Desiatynna Church ruins.
ⓐ Volodomyrska 2. ☎ 278 2924. ⏰ Thur–Tues 10.00–17.00.

National Art Museum

Built in the late 19th century in the style of a Greek temple, with six
large columns forming the portico, this holds a collection, in 21
galleries, largely unknown to the Western world. The works are
mainly by Ukrainian artists and include icons, paintings and
sculptures from the 14th century to the 20th century.
ⓐ Hrushevskoho 6. ☎ 278 7454. ⏰ Sat–Thur 10.00–18.00, Fri
11.00–19.00.

Museum of Russian Art

Housed in the former home of Fyodor Tereschenko, a sugar
millionaire, this small but luxurious mansion houses Kiev's greatest
collection of Russian art. An important piece is the icon of St George
slaying the dragon. The building also gives an idea of the lifestyle of
the wealthy in pre-Russian Revolution days.
ⓐ Tereschenkivska 9. ☎ 224 6218. ⏰ Fri–Tues 10.00–17.00.

Shevchenko National Opera and Ballet Theatre

The building is lavish, both inside and out, and the performances are
never less than grandiose. Completed in 1901, and designed in
Viennese style, it is one of the best preserved buildings in the city. It is
also the site of the assassination of the prime minister of Tsar
Nicholas II in 1911 in an abortive attempt to reform the government.
The only way to see the inside is to take in one of the performances,
but that's a good idea anyway.
ⓐ Volodomyrska 50. ☎ 224 7165, box office 229 1169.
ⓦ www.opera.com.ua. Ⓜ Metro: Zoloti Vorota.

RETAIL THERAPY

Khreschatyk (see page 70) is becoming one long strip mall, albeit very upmarket for the most part. International names such as Bally, Benetton, Nike and Reebok have stores on this street. There are also numerous local merchants selling quality jewellery, antiques and folk art. Fast food outlets, cafés and bars also line the street. There are many other good shops and shopping areas within one or two blocks of Khreschatyk.

Alta Centre was the first shopping mall in Kiev. It has a complete range of products for sale, from clothing and shoes, to sportswear, cosmetics and souvenirs. There are two department stores on site, a supermarket and several restaurants. Fashion Lab is a unique collection of boutiques featuring Ukrainian fashions. Most Saturdays there is a fashion show presenting work of Ukrainian designers. ⓐ Moskovsky prospekt 11A. ❶ 426 5454. ◐ Daily 10.00–22.00.

Bessarabsky Rynok (Market) is the place to buy the best quality fruit, vegetables and other foodstuffs. It is an open-air farmers' market, and worth visiting just to see how the locals shop for their daily diet. You can get free samples of many of the products. Sadly, most of the fruits and vegetables are now imported, with high prices. To find a true Ukrainian market, you will have to travel farther outside the city. ⓐ Bessarabska ploscha. ❶ 224 2317. ◐ Mon 08.00–17.00, Tues–Sun 08.00–20.00. ◎ Metro: Teatralna.

Globus is the underground shopping centre at Maidan Nezalezhnosti. The shops sell clothing, shoes, lingerie and accessories. Many designer labels, such as Esprit, Polo and Hilfiger, are represented. The shops open when the metro stations open, and close when the metro stations close. It is one of the best places to buy clothes in Kiev. ⓐ Maidan Nezalezhnosti. ① 238 5937. ⓛ Daily 05.30–24.00.

Mandarin Plaza is a seven-storey shopping centre with a full range of outlets. There are speciality boutiques of clothing designers from around the world, and a dedicated area for children. The plaza is quite posh – this is where the wealthy locals shop. ⓐ Baseina 4. ① 230 9591. ⓛ 10.00–22.00.

Metrograd Underground Shopping Complex is another underground shopping mall, but with much lower prices than Globus. You can buy just about anything here. ⓐ Under Bessarabska ploscha. ① 247 5665. ⓛ Daily 10.00–21.00.

TsUM (Central Universal Shop) is the old Russian-style department store, housed in a monolithic building. It is moving upmarket, and the residents of Kiev consider it to be their Harrods. Be that as it may, it is the best place to go to buy the basics. ⓐ vul Bohdana Khmelnytskoho 2. ① 224 9505. ⓛ Mon–Sat 09.00–20.00.

Ukrayina Department Store has recently been totally refurbished. There are five floors for shopping, a cinema, pharmacy, a bookstore and a 24-hour supermarket. ⓐ Peremohy 3. ① 496 1601. ⓛ Sun–Thur 10.00–21.00, Fri & Sat 10.00–22.00. Supermarket (separate entrance) daily 24 hours. ⓝ Metro: Vokzalna.

⦿ *Despite its economic problems, Kiev has some impressive shopping malls*

Art galleries

Atelier Karas A commercial art gallery that features contemporary works by local artists. ⓐ Andriivsky uzviz 22A. ⓣ 238 6531.

TAKING A BREAK

Baboon Book Coffee Shop is a combination coffee house and bookstore. The menu includes cakes, pastries, fruit cocktails and other desserts. The books are in English, Russian and Ukrainian. There is an exchange system for books and videotapes, and you can trade in your old books for other books or even for coffee and food. There are occasional live music programmes. ⓐ Khmelnytskoho 39. ⓣ 234 1503. ⓛ 09.00–02.00.

Butterfly is a quiet café near the Bessarabsky market. It is a downstairs room decorated with pictures of butterflies, serving affordable international and Ukrainian food. The speciality is *mlyntsa* (Ukrainian crepes). ⓐ Baseina 5B. ⓣ 244 9138. ⓛ Daily 11.00–23.00.

Coffeeum in Maidan is a two-storey coffee house in an old coffee/brandy/cigar bar dating back to about 1900. The coffee is good, and the decor is fascinating. ⓐ Maidan Nezalezhnosti. ⓣ 278 0490. ⓛ Daily 08.00–24.00.

Domashnya Kukhnya (Home Cooking) serves a great variety of Ukrainian food, along with hot and cold drinks, including beer. It is cafeteria-style, but the quality is good, and the prices low, which is why it becomes noisy and crowded at main mealtimes and at weekends.
ⓐ Khmelnytskoho 16/22. ⓣ 234 2918. ⓛ Daily 08.00–23.00.

Fresh Bar is one for the health-food freaks. Near the Lenin monument, it serves salads and juices and other healthy food containing the kinds of vitamins and minerals we should be eating. It also serves a variety of very good desserts, albeit of the low-calorie variety. ❷ Tarasa Shevchenka bulv 1. ❶ 235 3751. ❸ Daily 11.00–22.00.

Kaffa is a smoke-free café, rare in Kiev. It is very popular, and serves a wide variety of very tasty, caffeine-rich coffees. The menu is rather long, and the service good but slow. The interior is decorated in an African motif, with masks, beads and leather. ❷ Tarasa Shevchenka prov. 3. ❶ 464 0505. ❸ Mon 11.00–23.00, Tues–Fri 09.00–23.00, Sat & Sun 10.00–23.00.

Marquise de Chocolat is one for chocoholics. The interior is dark red velvet, with soft sofas and roses and apples on each table; some of the decorations are a bit over the top. Although hot chocolate is a speciality, they also serve coffees, teas and all kinds of chocolate desserts. ❷ Prorizna 4 (upstairs). ❶ 228 6590. ❸ Daily 12.00–23.00.

McDonald's The golden arches have reached Kiev, and there are several locations about the city. Despite some local disdain for such American icons, these fast-food outlets are very busy. The menu is quite small compared to McDonald's in Western countries and there is no breakfast. Although the cloakrooms are built to Western standards, they are so busy that they are not always kept as clean as they should be. ❷ Khreschatyk 19A. ❶ 230 2737. ❸ Daily 07.00–23.00.

Nescafé The well known international brand has opened three coffee shops in Kiev. They serve a wide variety of coffees, including cappuccinos, espressos and iced coffees at reasonable prices.

The menu also includes salads, sandwiches and desserts. The decor is bright and modern. ❸ Velyka Zhytomyrska 8A. ❶ 462 0809. ❶ Daily 10.00–23.00.

Puzata Khata (Paunchy House) specialises in Ukrainian food. If you are on a diet, take the name of the place seriously, as this place will send the calorie count sky-high. Housed in an authentic peasant house, the lower floor serves main courses, while the second floor specialises in pastries. Breakfast, lunch and dinner are served, and it is a good place to try out authentic Ukrainian food at low prices. ❸ Baseina 1/2. ❶ 246 7245. ❶ Daily 08.00–23.00.

Rostiks is Kiev's answer to Kentucky Fried Chicken. The menu includes chicken, French fries and even corn-on-the-cob. ❸ There are three locations, Globus and Metrograd shopping malls, and Respublikansky Stadion metro station. ❶ 227 3775. ❶ Daily 10.00–22.00.

Schvydko is Kiev's version of McDonald's. Fast food, borscht, *varenyky*, chicken Kiev and salads are on your plate quickly. They also serve hot and cold drinks and beer and there is a children's menu. ❸ Maidan Nezalezhnosti. ❶ 278 6409. ❶ Daily 08.00–23.00.

AFTER DARK

There is no shortage of restaurants, bars, discos and nightclubs and casinos in the city centre. Kiev has embraced many aspects of Western culture wholeheartedly, with prices to match. You should be able to find just about any type of food you want, and any type of entertainment , from disco to ballet, chamber music to roulette, cinemas to strippers.

Restaurants

Dining at the cafés listed under 'Taking a break' will save on your wallet, but if you are looking for fine food, try one of the following establishments.

Concord HH–HHH A rooftop restaurant that has good views of the city. The menu offers an eclectic variety of dishes and styles, from French rabbit to Indonesian fish to Moroccan lamb.
ⓐ Pushkinska 42–44. ❶ 244 1235. Ⓝ Metro: Ploscha Lva Tolsovo.

Fellini HH–HHH Serves a mixture of French and Italian dishes.
ⓐ Horodetskoho 5 ❶ 229 5462. Ⓝ Metro: Maidan Nezalezhnosti.

Za Dvoma Zaytsamy HH–HHH The name means 'Chasing Two Hares', and the restaurant is named after a cult film of the same name based on a Ukrainian proverb that says if you chase two hares, you will catch neither. The decor is 19th-century and the food is very good Ukrainian at a reasonable price. Of course, the menu includes some rabbit dishes. ⓐ Andriivsky uzviz 34. ❶ 229 7972.

Empire HHH–HHH+ The restaurant on the 18th floor of the Premier Palace Hotel serves both Ukrainian and European cuisine. Both the food and the panoramic view of the city are excellent. ⓐ Tarasa Shevchenka 5–7 (8th Floor). ❶ 244 1235. Ⓝ Metro: Teatralna.

Lypsky Osobnyak HHH–HHH+ This place is reputed to serve the finest Ukrainian food in the city, raising traditional peasant fare to the level of haute cuisine. This is another restaurant featuring fine 19th-century decor and offers excellent service and a large wine cellar. ⓐ Lypska 15. ❶ 254 0090. Ⓝ Metro: Arsenalna.

Bars & clubs

Art Club 44 Primarily a cellar jazz club, but other music is played. Unpretentious, it is usually crowded. There is a cover charge, and drinks are expensive. ❸ Kreshchatyk 44. ❶ 229 4137. Ⓝ Metro: Teatralna.

Eric's Bierstube German-style beer hall located in a basement, catering for wealthier clients. The beer is good but pricey. ❸ Chervonoarmiyska 20. ❶ 235 9472. Ⓝ Metro: Ploscha Lva Tolsovo.

Golden Gate Typical Irish pub featuring great pub food, draught beer and Irish whiskey. It also opens for a high-cholesterol breakfast at 08.00. ❸ Volodomyrska 40–42. ❶ 235 5188. Ⓝ Metro: Zoloti Vorota.

O'Brien's Irish Pub This is a good place to have a good expat time. Reputed to have no class and cheap bands, but it is still a good meeting place. ❸ Mykhaylivska 17A. ❶ 229 1 584. Ⓝ Metro: Maidan Nezalezhnosti.

Opium Dance Club Caters to a young, hip, hard-core rave crowd, and has room for 1500 dancers. It is connected to the Imperial Casino (see next page). ❸ Saksahanskovo 1. ❶ 205 5393. Ⓝ Metro: Respublikansy Stadion.

Tchaikovsky A popular local disco club, with more of an accent on glamour than Opium Dance Club. There is a cover charge for men, but women are admitted free. ❸ Bessarabska 1. ❶ 234 7406. Ⓝ Metro: Teatralna.

◖ *The Independence Monument dominates Maidan Nezalezhnosti by night*

Casinos

Casino 21st Century Currently a very popular venue. specialising in poker. ➋ Saksahanskovo 51. ☎ 220 1703. Ⓜ Metro: Respublikansy Stadion.

Imperial Casino Garishly done out in pinks and golds, this is a classic-style casino with the emphasis on its roulette tables. ➋ Saksahanskovo 1. ☎ 224 3957. Ⓜ Metro: Respublikansy Stadion.

Metro Jackpot This is the place to find slot machiness – lots of them. ➋ Mecknikova 14. ☎ 234 7934. Ⓜ Metro: Klovska.

Classical music & theatre

Almost all performances are in Ukrainian or Russian, with the exception of the operas, which are performed in their original languages. However, it is worthwhile to attend a performance to see the lavish costumes and scenery, and to feel the reaction of the audience.

Taras Shevchenko National Opera of Ukraine No trip to Kiev would be complete without attending a performance at the Opera House, where both opera and ballet are performed. The productions are second to none, and the venue is also world-class (see page 78). Even if these kinds of entertainment are not your thing, it is a Ukrainian thing, so you should do it. There are performances just about every night starting at about 17.00, as well as matinées on many days at 12.00. Prices are low, starting around 20Hr., but you may want to pay more in order to get good seats. Just do it!
➋ Volodomyrska 50. ☎ 224 7165, box office 229 1169. Ⓦ www.opera.com.ua Ⓜ Metro: Zoloti Vorota.

House of Organ and Chamber Music Hosts classical concerts inside the century-old, Gothic-style St Nicholas cathedral.
Ⓐ Chervonoarmiyska 77. ⓣ 528 3186. Ⓦ www.organhall.kiev.ua

National Philharmonic Ukraine's national orchestra gives regular concerts, as well as holding international music competitions and festivals. Its home is a beautiful building that was once the headquarters of the Kiev Merchants' Assembly. Ⓐ Volodymyrskya 2. ⓣ 278 1697. Ⓦ www.filarmonia.com.ua

Palace of Sport Although primarily used for sporting events, this is also a regular venue for Ukrainian and international rock and pop concerts. Ⓐ Sportyvna pl. 1. ⓣ 246 7406.

Cinemas
There are only two cinemas in central Kiev that show films in their original English:

Kyiv Ⓐ Chervonoarmiyska 19. ⓣ 23 47 381. Ⓦ www.kievkino.com.ua
Ⓝ Metro: Ploscha Lva Toltovo.

Odesa Ⓐ Peremohy prospekt 3. ⓣ 496 15 11. Ⓦ www.kinoodessa.com
Ⓝ Metro: Vokzalna.

Pechersk

Pechersk means 'of the caves', and is the old, historic heart of Kiev. The building of the caves started in 1051 and the construction of the first surface building followed shortly after. The area developed to make Kiev the cultural and spiritual centre of Slavic Christianity from ancient times up to the Russian Revolution.

SIGHTS & ATTRACTIONS

Kievo-Pecherska Lavra (The Caves Monastery)

Kiev's top tourist attraction is in fact many attractions in one. Besides the caves, there are several museums and many churches. There is a general admission to the Upper Lavra site, and then individual admissions to many of the churches and museums, as well as an extra charge if you want to take pictures. This can add up, so you may want to consider using a guided tour, or even a personal guide. Admission to the Lower Lavra and caves themselves is free, which the guides are reluctant to tell you.

Although the site, with the exception of the Lower Lavra and the caves themselves which belong to the church, is officially a government-owned Historical and Cultural Preserve, it is also a religious shrine of the Ukrainian Orthodox Church, under the authority of the Moscow Patriarch. Every year tens of thousands of devout Orthodox Christians make the pilgrimage to pray at the Lavra, considered the spiritual heart of the country. Visitors should treat this as a very holy site, and act with the appropriate reverence and respect. Unfortunately, tourism and capitalism are catching up. Souvenir shops and other devices to separate visitors from their money are starting to pervade the site.

Visiting the caves is a very moving experience, even for the non-believer. However, if you are claustrophobic, do not even think of entering, as the caves are barely 2 m (6 ft) high, and less than 1 m (3 ft) wide. Although the entrance is free, you should consider taking a guided tour, as they do not make it easy for an independent traveller to find the exact entrance spot. It is customary to purchase a candle when entering, and as the cost is only a few hryvnia, you should do so. Photography is not allowed, talking should only be done in whispers, women are expected to cover their heads, and men are expected to remove their hats. Due to the popularity of the site, try to avoid weekends, or if you can only visit at a weekend, go early. Many sections of the caves are now blocked off and reserved for the use of monks and true pilgrims only.

The restored Dormition Cathedral is the monastery's centrepiece

THE HISTORY OF THE CAVES MONASTERY

A *lavra* is a major monastery of the Eastern (Orthodox) Church, headed by an Archimandrite, the equivalent of an abbot in the Western Church. The Kyivian Lavra was founded by the Russian monk later to be known as St Anthony of the Caves, who had taken his vows at the famous monastery of Athos in Greece, in the mid-11th century.

The cave he occupied had been previously inhabited by Ilarion, who later became the first Metropolitan of Kyiv. The first monks excavated more caves and built a church above them. The monastery attracted powerful and wealthy patrons and soon became the largest religious and cultural centre in what is now Ukraine.

The monastery was a target for envious invaders, including the Mongols and the Tatars, and was sacked and destroyed several times, but arose again on each occasion. It became an important educational and cultural centre and in the 17th century housed the first printing press in Ukraine.

Repression continued, by both the imperial authorities of Russia (who confiscated the enormous property – including three cities and seven towns – owned by the monastery as a result of gifts from its patrons) and later the Soviets, who seized most of the relics and precious artefacts and attempted to turn the site into a centre for anti-religious propaganda. In 1941 the retreating Russian forces blew up the entire complex as the German army entered Kiev.

After World War II the Soviet authorities allowed the reinstitution of the *lavra* and the site was restored.

The Near Caves were started by St Anthony, who as a hermit did not take to the communal life of the main monastery he had helped to found in the original (Far) caves. He is buried here, as are over 120 other monks. There are three churches down here, including the Vedenska Church, famous for its gold icons. The entrance is through the Khrestovozdvyzhenska Church (Church of the Raising of the Cross), built in 1700.

The Far Caves entrance is connected to the Near Caves exit by a covered walkway. The Far Caves are the original underground monastery started by St Anthony and his successor, St Theodosius. These caves also have three underground churches, as well as the remains of many mummified monks. The entrance is in the Annozachatiyivskaya Church (Church of the Conception of St Anne), built in 1679.

The Troitskaya (Trinity Gate) Church is now used as the main entrance to the Lavra. It was built in 1108, and features interesting murals, painted in 1900, on its outside walls. The Great Bell Tower is nearly 100 m (300 ft) tall, the world's tallest Orthodox building. If you want a panoramic view of the Lavra, and most of Kiev, you can climb the nearly 200 steps to the top. Be careful, as the steps and guardrail are not as safe as they should be.

The Dormition Cathedral (Church of the Assumption) was originally built in 1077, and is technically the oldest above-ground church in the Lavra. The original was destroyed in World War II, but rebuilt by the city of Kiev in 1998–2000. It features seven beautiful gold domes, and is the resting place of St Theodosius.

There are many other religious sites at the Lavra, including the Church of All Saints, the Chapel of St Anthony and St Theodosius,

---

▶ *Khrestovozdvyzhenska Church is the impressive entrance to the Near Caves*

● *Even without visiting the caves, you could fill a day's sightseeing at the Kievo-Pechersk Lavra*

the St Nicholas Church, the Refectory, the monks' dormitories, the Church of the Nativity of the Virgin (1696), and the Bell Tower of the Far Caves (1761).

ⓐ Sichnevoho Povstannya 21. ☎ 290 3071. ● Upper Lavra 09.30–18.00; Lower Lavra sunrise–sunset; Caves 08.30–16.30. Ⓦ www.lavra.kiev.ua Ⓝ Metro: Arsenalna, then bus 20.

Museum of the Great Patriotic War

This is located just south of the Caves Monastery. It is a memorial complex dedicated to the Ukrainian struggle against the Nazis in World War II. The panoramas and exhibits are quite sobering. The focal point of the museum is a 62 m (200 ft) high statue of a female warrior called Rodyna Mat (the Nation's Mother). Referred to as the 'Iron Maiden', she is actually built of titanium. It is possible to take an elevator or stairs up to her right hand, where there is a viewing platform. In the park grounds surrounding the museum there is statuary, the Eternal Flame, the Tomb of the Unknown Soldier, and displays of military equipment such as tanks and aircraft.

ⓐ Sichnevoho Povstannia 44. ❶ 285 9452. ❶ Tues–Sun 10.00–17.00.
Ⓜ Metro: Arsenalna, then bus 20.

Central Botanical Gardens

This park lies along the banks of the River Dnepr and was opened in 1936. It features over 13,000 trees, bushes and other plants from five continents. It was once owned by the nearby Vydubytsky Monastery, and there are spectacular views of the gardens and river from the monastery.

ⓐ Tymiryazievska 1. ❶ 295 4527. ❶ Daily 09.30–17.00.
Ⓜ Metro:Druzhby Narodiv.

Vydubytsky Monastery

The monastery was founded in the 10th century, with St Michael's Church being built in 1070. Legend has it that after Prince Vladimir made Kiev Christian, he cut down the pagan idol, Perun, and tossed it into the river, where it should have sunk. It did not, and at the spot where it floated ashore the monastery was established. The monastery is located at the narrowest part of the river, and for years controlled the ferry crossing here. This monastery was also the site of much of the early writing on the history of Russia and Ukraine. Although the monastery was virtually destroyed by the Soviet regime, some of the early mosaics, frescoes and architectural features still exist. It was re-established in 1998.

🅐 Timiryazevska 1. Ⓝ Metro:Druzhby Narodiv.

RETAIL THERAPY

Silk Route is an upmarket souvenir store near the Caves Monastery. It sells many beautiful, elaborate and artistic items. 🅐 Suvorova 4.
🆃 295 0324. 🕒 Daily 10.00–20.00.

TAKING A BREAK

Coffeeum in Pechersk is a new, two-level coffee house near the Caves Monastery. Photo exhibitions line the walls. 🅐 Sichnevoho Povstannia 3. 🆃 290 5796. 🕒 Daily 08.00–24.00.

AFTER DARK

There is very little nightlife in Pechersk, which other than the Caves and some other attractions is mainly a residential area.
One restaurant in this area stands out, though.

Marokana Restaurant HHH Serving international cuisine with an oriental twist, this caters to Kiev's wealthier set. 🅐 Lesi Ukrayinky 24.
🆃 254 4999. Ⓝ Metro: Pecherska.

🅞 *Vydubytsky Monastery has a 1000-year history*

Podil

Podil was originally the river port of Kiev, and the place where the craftsmen and foreign merchants lived. It is on the River Dnepr plain, below the rest of the city, which sits on the hills above. The area was destroyed by fire in 1811 but subsequently rebuilt. Amazingly, Podil survived the Soviet repression and World War II intact, so that today the area still looks much as it did in the 19th century. In addition to the specific attractions listed below, the whole area is worth visiting for its historic buildings, small churches, synagogue and old merchants' homes. Today it is becoming gentrified as young professionals are moving in, and has many boutiques and fine restaurants.

SIGHTS & ATTRACTIONS

Funicular

Connecting Podil with the city centre, this provides an alternative route to Podil from the one via Andrew's Descent. The view is good, and the cost is only 50 kopecks. You should consider walking down Andrew's Descent, exploring the streets of Podil, and then taking the funicular back up the hill to the city centre. The bottom end of the funicular is near the boat terminal, while the top end is behind St Michael's Monastery.

National Museum of Chernobyl

You can almost feel that you are at the site of the disaster caused by the explosion of the Number 4 nuclear reactor in April 1986 (see page 112). Road signs from towns and villages near Chernobyl are used, as are old computers and other exhibits with 'don't touch'

signs. Many of the exhibits are graphic and haunting, and may be scary for children. The most emotional is the film of the firemen who went in to clean up just after the accident, most of whom died within weeks due to radioactive poisoning. Opened in 1993, the museum has not been very well maintained, and normally has few visitors. English-speaking guides are available.

🅐 Khoryva provulok 1. ☎ 417 5427. ⏰ Mon–Fri 10.00–18.00, Sat 10.00–17.00. Ⓜ Metro: Kontraktova Ploscha.

Kontraktova ploscha (Contract Square)

You are at the centre of Podil here. It features an open market place, with shopping arcades that were built about 200 years ago. On one side is the Hostiny Dvor (Hospice Court), and on the other is the Contract House, formerly the offices for the market place.

Ⓜ Metro: Kontraktova Ploscha.

Museum of One Street

This fascinating little museum stands at the bottom of Andrew's Descent. It tells the history of this street through the years, with emphasis on the period just before the Russian Revolution. Its collection of simple artefacts such as cloths, eyeglasses, dishes and books are displayed in such a way that you get a real feel for how people actually lived here.

🅐 Andriivsky uzviz 2B. ☎ 425 0398. Ⓜ Metro: Kontraktova Ploscha.

CCA (The Soros Center of Contemporary Art)

This is located at the Kiev-Mohyla Akademy. It is part of an

◀ *St Andrew's Church is the start of the Descent (Andriivsky uzviz) that leads visitors into Podil*

international contemporary art network that promotes contact between artists, and gives them a forum to display their works. The works of many contemporary artists, both local and international, are on display.

🅐 Skovorody 2. ☎ 238 24 46. 🆆 www.cca.kiev.ua 🕐 Tues–Sun 13.00–18.00.

CULTURE

Podil Drama Theatre

The theatre performs everything from light local works to Shakespeare and the performances generally are very entertaining.

🅐 Kontraktova Ploscha 4. ☎ 416 5489. Ⓜ Metro: Kontraktova Ploscha.

Marionette Theatre

Puppetry is considered an art form in this part of the world and puppet shows are enjoyed by young and old alike. The Marionette Theatre is well known for recreating classical Ukrainian fairy tales with its puppets.

🅐 Sahaydachnovo 29/3. ☎ 417 3058. Ⓜ Metro: Poshtova Ploscha.

TAKING A BREAK

Kaffa Another branch of Kiev's smoke-free chain of cafés (see page 83). 🅐 Skovorody 5. ☎ 464 0505. 🕐 Mon 11.00–23.00, Tues–Fri 09.00–23.00, Sat & Sun 10.00–23.00.

Chayniy Club is a small café much frequented by old ladies gossiping over tea. Over 60 varieties of tea are served, including one for every sign on the zodiac. Business lunches are served, and there

is also a menu of Jewish cuisine, including kosher dishes.
🅐 Mezhyhirska 22. 🕿 425 1977. 🕒 Daily 10.00–23.00.

Domashnya Kukhnya (Home Cooking) The Podil branch of this
establishment is very similar to that in the city centre (see page 82)
– good Ukrainian food, if a trifle noisy. 🅐 Kostiantynivska 2A. 🕿 467
6048. 🕒 Daily 08.00–23.00.

AFTER DARK

Restaurants

Arizona HH This typical American-style steak house is a favourite of
the locals, and as been around for a long time. 🅐 Naberezhno-
Khreshchatytska 25. 🕿 425 24387. Ⓜ Metro: Kontraktova Ploscha.

El Asador HH Like Arizona, this is a steak house, although this one is
Argentinian, and quite new. 🅐 Nyzhniy Val 29. 🕿 425 4402.
Ⓜ Metro: Kontraktova Ploscha.

Khutorok HH–HHH A wooden paddle steamer converted to a
floating restaurant. You can sit outside on the deck in summer, or
huddle near the fireplace inside in winter. The menu is typically
Ukrainian, but there are vegetarian starters. 🅐 Berth 1, Naberezhno-
Khreshchatytska. 🕿 460 7019. Ⓜ Metro: Kontraktova Ploscha.

Mandarin HH–HHH Chinese-style riverboat moored on the Dnepr. It
serves good Chinese (and Japanese) food. 🅐 Berth 6, Naberezhno-
Khreshchatytska. 🕿 459 0877. Ⓜ Metro: Kontraktova Ploscha.

Minimo HH–HHH Considered one of the best restaurants in the city,

its theme is based on a Soviet cult movie of the same name. Cuisine is Georgian, and features mainly lamb dishes, many very spicy. A vegetarian menu is also available. ❸ Spaska 10A. ❶ 417 3545. Ⓜ Metro: Kontraktova Ploscha.

Marrakech HH–HHH As its name implies, this restaurant has an Arabian theme. The menu is mainly couscous dishes, although not as spicy as one would find in the real Marrakech. ❸ Petra Sahaydachnoho 24. ❶ 494 0494. Ⓜ Metro: Kontraktova Ploscha.

Haiffa HHH–HHH+ A Jewish restaurant that serves favourite Israeli dishes, as well as traditional Ukrainian-Jewish food.
❸ Kostyantynivska 57. ❶ 417 2512. Ⓜ Metro: Tarasa Shevchenka.

L'Amour HHH–HHH+ Serves French cuisine prepared by a gourmet chef. It is housed in a quaint French-looking cottage next to the River Dnepr. The fish, especially the tuna, is very good.
❸ Naberezhno-Khreschatytskaya 16/17. ❶ 451 5080. Ⓜ Metro: Kontraktova Ploscha.

Bars & clubs

ModaBar A small ship converted to a night club. Moored near the Mandarin Restaurant, it claims to have the longest bar in Europe. It features pop music, and fashion shows on a transparent catwalk. Admission is free, but drinks are expensive. ❸ Berth 6, Naberezhno-Khreshchatytska. ❶ 428 7388. Ⓜ Metro: Kontraktova Ploscha.

◐ *The reconstructed synagogue is a reminder that Podil was a centre of Kiev's large pre-war Jewish population*

Around Kiev

Outside the central areas of the city, Kiev sprawls in massive suburbs in all directions. The homes tend to be small and nondescript. Other than the attractions listed here, there is very little for a visitor to see and do. The Turist Hotel complex on the left bank of the Dnepr has good restaurants, bars and nightclubs. See the main city map (pages 62–63) for sights in greater Kiev.

SIGHTS & ATTRACTIONS

Babi Yar

This sobering site is dedicated to the memory of the tens of thousands of citizens, mainly Jewish, who were massacred here by

● *The moving Children's Memorial at Babi Yar*

the Nazis in World War II. From 29 to 31 September 1941 some 34,000 Jews were killed here, as were many more 'enemies of the Third Reich' during the rest of the Nazi occupation: in all, over 100,000 victims are believed to be buried here. During the 1970s the Soviets erected a monument to the citizens who perished and since independence in 1991 the construction of memorials has begun. **The Children's Memorial**, dedicated to the children who died here, and

JEWISH KIEV

Jews have played an important part in the history and culture of Kiev. One of the oldest documents in Kiev is written in Hebrew. From the 12th to the 19th century Jews played prominent roles in the political, cultural, business and scientific communities of Kiev. Sadly, as in many other parts of the world, the Jews became scapegoats in times of war and unrest. The Cossacks, Tsars, Communists and Nazis all persecuted the Jews. Before World War II Jews made up about 20 per cent of Kiev's population. Today it is only 3 per cent, but growing. Since independence, the Central Synagogue, in the city centre, and the Podil Synagogue have been returned to their rightful owners and have been rebuilt as places for Jews to worship. Golda Meir, former Prime Minister of Israel, was born in Kiev at Baseina 5A, before she emigrated to the United States with her family. There is a bust and a plaque dedicated to her at this address. Sholom Aleichem, a famous storyteller and author, was born just outside Kiev, and there is a monument to him at Rognidynska 3. His writings inspired *Fiddler on the Roof*.

the **Menorah Monument**, placed on the actual execution site, are grim and chilling reminders of what happened here. There is a large Jewish cemetery nearby.

Ⓝ Metro: Dorohozhychi.

Pyrohovo Museum of Folk Architecture and Life

Located about 12 km (8 miles) south of Kiev in the town of Pyrohovo, this large open-air museum is made up of over 300 buildings dating back to the 16th century. These authentic buildings have been collected from all over Ukraine to form a 'village' depicting life in older times. Different areas of the museum depict different areas of Ukraine. Here you will see barns, schools, homes, churches, windmills and other such buildings. Inside the buildings are exhibits such as stoves, clothing, ceramics, household utensils and farm equipment. Roaming the property are actors dressed as peasants, who answer questions and engage in traditional peasant activities such as wood-carving, pottery-making, bee-keeping and embroidery. On Sundays a traditional church service is held in one of the churches on site. Traditional Ukrainian meals are served at several locations. You'll get more out of it if you take a guided tour with one of the English-speaking guides.

ⓐ Chervonopraporna, Pyrohovo. ① 266 5542. ⓒ Daily 10.00–17.00.
Ⓝ Metro: Lybidska, then bus 27; or Metro: Respublikansky Stadion, then *marshrutka* 156.

Pokrovska Convent

The convent was founded by the sister-in-law of Tsar Alexander II when she recovered from an illness after visiting the Caves

▶ *St Nikolai's Cathedral is one of the jewels of the Pokrovska Convent*

Monastery. **The Pokrovska Church**, which looks like a cake decorated in pink, was built in 1889. **St Nikolai's Cathedral**, in white, blue and green, was built in 1911. Both are designed in pure Tsarist Russian style. The convent was far enough out of town to avoid any desecration during the wars and turmoil of the 20th century.

📍 Bekhteryevsky 15. ☎ 211 3825. Ⓜ Metro: Lukyanivska.

Chernobyl (Chornobyl)

This is the site of the world's worst nuclear disaster, 128 km (80 miles) from Kiev. There is not a lot to see there, but it is more of a 'been there, done that' type of destination for the curious. The radiation levels are now quite low, so visitors do not have to fear for their health. Desolate and overgrown landscapes and eerie empty villages are mostly what you see, along with the massive concrete cap poured

NUCLEAR DISASTER

Early in the morning of 26 April 1986, the Number 4 reactor at the Chernobyl power plant exploded, sending its 500-tonne top and 9 tonnes of radioactive material into the sky. Nearly 100 times the radioactive material produced by the Hiroshima bomb blew west and north, leaving devastation in its path, contaminating over 35,000 sq km of forest and farmland. Six days later, the wind would turn south and carry the radioactive cloud over an unsuspecting Kiev during the May Day celebrations.

Ironically, this nuclear explosion was the result of a safety test. The reactor was being taken down for maintenance on 25 April when the operators decided to test the emergency shutdown system. Due to operational errors, as well as a design flaw, the reactor overheated, resulting in a steam explosion, followed by the nuclear explosion.

The Soviets tried to cover up the accident, but when the radioactive cloud reached Sweden, Swedish scientists alerted the world. After the accident, the reactor and other radioactive material were covered in a large steel and concrete 'sarcophagus'. The cover is now disintegrating, but a new cover is being prepared with international assistance.

Only two people died in the initial accident, but sadly 29 firemen were immediately sent in to clean up the mess. They were not given proper information or safety gear, and all died within weeks due to radiation poisoning. Since then, an estimated 5000 more people have died as a result of the accident, and up to a million more people may be affected in the long term by cancer, birth defects, heart disease and suicide. The aftermath of this disaster will continue to haunt Ukraine and Kiev for many years to come.

over the remains of the reactor. Visiting Chernobyl as an individual is not easy, as there is no regular transport, and there is a lot of red tape to clear in order to visit the site. Under-18s are prohibited. Taking a guided package tour is preferable and takes all the hassle out of the visit. Costs for an individual trip are high, but decrease as the number in the group increases, with a group of ten or more getting the best deal. Some tour companies going to Chernobyl are:

SAM 🄲 Ivana Franka 40B. ☎ 238 2060. 🌐 www.sam.com.ua/eng
New Logic 🄲 Mikhailivska 6A. ☎ 462 0462. 🌐 www.newlogic.com.ua

Pereyaslav Khmelnytsky & Pereyaslav Historical Preserve

Pereyaslav Khmelnytsky is about 90 minutes south of Kiev on the left bank of the River Dnepr. The city was important in Kyivian Rus times, but fell out of favour after Bohdan Khmelnytsky signed Ukraine over to the Tsars in 1654. Jewish writer Sholom Aleichem was born here, and there is a museum dedicated to him in the city. This is a good place to learn about Kyivian Rus, Cossacks and everyday life in rural Ukraine. There is a museum of folk architecture, similar to the one in Kiev, as well as the beautiful Church of St Michael. There is a regular bus service from Kiev, but you may find it easier to take a packaged tour.

Bila Tserkva

The name means 'white church', and this city, about an hour south of Kiev, is known for its many small white churches and beautiful parks. It gained its place in Ukrainian history thanks to Bohdan Khmelnytsky, who signed a treaty with Poland here in 1651, which made big concessions to the Poles. Within a year, Khmelnytsky broke the treaty, and drove the Poles out. There is a regular bus service from Kiev, but an organised tour is less hassle.

RETAIL THERAPY

There are two open markets in the suburbs located adjacent to metro stations. Both are well established, and you will find shoppers digging through piles of goods, most of which have been shipped in from Italy or Turkey. Bargaining is recommended. One is located at the Druzhby Norodiv metro station south of the city centre, and the other is located at the Shulyavska station west of the city centre.

⬤ *Cosmoplitan Odessa is well within reach of Kiev for a weekend*

Lviv (Lvov)

Lviv, also spelt Lvov on English-language maps, once the sister city of Warsaw and Krakow, is rapidly emerging as Ukraine's second city. It has the untouched quality that Prague once had before it attracted hordes of tourists. This architectural and historical gem will have you singing its praises.

Founded by Prince Danylo Halystsky in the mid-13th century, it was named for his son Lev. Many of the city's buildings still survive from that era. Lviv is an architectural time capsule, with buildings and churches representing periods from the 13th to the 21th century. The heart of the city is the elegant Market Square, built and developed during the 16th–18th centuries. Each of the 44 houses around the square is unique and has its own story to tell. No wonder UNESCO has added this area to its World Heritage List.

Getting from Kiev to Lviv is easy, with many options. The least expensive is to take the bus or the train, with several departures daily. Cost of the bus is under 60Hr. one way, and travel takes from 9 to 11 hours, depending on traffic and weather. Perhaps the best way to take the train is to take the overnight luxury express, for about 200Hr. one way. There are also several daily flights between Kiev and Lviv: the cost is about 1200Hr. return and flight time is about 90 minutes.

SIGHTS & ATTRACTIONS

Rynok ploscha (Market Square)

Rynok ploshcha is the epicentre of Lviv's architectural heritage. A fire nearly destroyed the square in the 16th century but it was rebuilt. In fact, over the centuries this square has been a work in progress.

Highlights of the square, declared a World Heritage Site by UNESCO in 1998, include the 19th-century town hall with its neo-Renaissance tower, House No. 4, the Bandanelli Palace (also called the Black Mansion), with its striking facade, built for an Italian merchant; House No. 6, the Kornyakt House (also known as the Royal Mansion), with its row of sculpted knights along the rooftop; the Boyim Chapel, the burial chapel of a Hungarian merchant, and the Roman Catholic Cathedral, visited by Pope John Paul II in 2001.

Bandanelli Palace Museum

This is supposed to be the Museum of the History of the Postal Service, but you won't find much in the way of postal exhibits. What you will find is the beautifully restored palace of Signor Bandanelli, who in 1629 began a mail service in the city – hence the postal museum . The newly opened interior houses a mixed bag of civic paraphernalia, with a pottery collection on the second floor.

📍 Rynok ploshcha 2. 🕐 Mon–Fri 09.00–17.00, Sat & Sun 10.00–1700.

Royal Mansion & Historical Museum

Take a step back in time at Lviv's Historical Museum, the aptly titled Royal Mansion. This was once a family residence of dashing Polish monarch Jan Sisisky. The famed Italianate courtyard is a pleasant place to wander around. Once you are inside, all traces of the 21st century evaporate. Portraits of gallant heroes line the walls and you can well imagine some prince waltzing through the salons with his comely young princess.

📍 Rynok ploshcha 6. 📞 (322) 749061. 🕐 Mon–Fri 10.00–17.00, Sat & Sun 12.00–17.00.

▶ *Lviv's majestic Opera House dates from its Austro-Hungarian era*

Dzyga Cultural Museum

The gallery here is the centre of modern art in Lviv. Not only are the exhibits worth the trip, you can also enjoy one of the best bars in town. Besides a vibrant gallery of contemporary art (stashed away in the quarters of the former Dominican monastery), Dzyga also hosts a theatre studio and workshops for children.

ⓐ Virmenska 35. ⓣ (322) 75201. ⓛ Daily 10.00–17.00.

Lviv Gallery of Art

This is likely to be a highlight of any culture vulture's trip to town. There is a stunning array of treasures to view, with impressive offerings from Italian, Dutch, French and Spanish Schools. Perhaps most interesting of all are the paintings from pre-World War I Galicia. A great flowering of art took place in the region during that era, with artists such as Mehoffer, Wyspianski and Malczewski all stunning the critics.

ⓐ Stefanyka 3. ⓣ (322) 723948. ⓛ Daily 10.00–18.00.

Lviv Opera House

The counts and countesses may have long since departed but the grandeur of this place still makes a powerful impact. You'd pay an arm and a leg for a seat in such a marvel in Western Europe. And even if you're not bowled over by the performance, the tickets won't break the bank, so you're unlikely to kick yourself for having made the effort. The dazzling opera house was founded in 1897 and it can seat as many as a thousand. Don't miss the Hall of Mirrors upstairs.

ⓐ Svobody prospekt 28. ⓛ During performance hours – varies.

Apteka (Pharmacy) Museum

Step inside the door and you will find yourself in one of the most beautiful places in Lviv. This Renaissance-era townhouse has more than half-a-dozen rooms to explore that will immerse you in a bygone culture. The pharmacy, now housed in the main room, has been conjuring up remedies and potions since 1735. Be sure not to miss the courtyard at the back.

🅰 Drukarska 2. ☎ (322) 720041. 🕐 Mon–Fri 09.00–17.00, Sat & Sun 10.00–17.00.

RETAIL THERAPY

Bam Pronounce the name as 'Vam' and head here for all the essentials you will need to keep you going for a picnic or for a week or longer. The array of sausage options is positively astonishing.
🅰 Vygovskogo 100. 🕐 Daily 09.00–22.00.

Folk Art Market Just around the corner from the National Opera you will find this treasure trove of handicraft and folk art. Potter around the stalls and you are sure to discover some treasure you simply cannot do without, such as an embroidered Cossack shirt. Be prepared to bargain and don't be put off if the seller seems to ask a suspiciously large amount at first. 🅰 Vicheva ploscha. 🕐 Daily 09.00–17.00.

Letter Bookshop Book-lovers should head for the orange house off the south-western corner of Rynok ploscha. There you will find one of the best bookshops in town. There is a good range of titles in English, including guidebooks to the city as well as glossy coffee-table souvenirs to pore over once you get back home. The delicious snacks and very decent coffee in the cosy little café alongside may keep you longer than you expected. 🅰 Shevska 6. 🕐 Daily 09.00–22.00.

Switoch There should be a very large warning label on the door – 'Careful! calories inside!' Switoch is Ukraine's leading chocolate firm. The principal Lviv outlet is housed in the mansion that was once the home of the legendary Polish confectionery company Zalewski. Inside you can still find many of the pre-war art deco furnishings. Besides more chocolates than you could possibly count, you'll find this is a good spot to pick up some other local delights, such as the highly prized Niemiroff honey vodka and other tasty liqueurs. **ⓐ** Shevchenka prospekt 10. **ⓣ** (322) 726741. **ⓛ** Daily 09.00–17.00.

Services
Aval Bank is an easy-to-find multi-service bank adjacent to the main post office. **ⓐ** Slovatsky 1. **ⓣ** 8 800 500 5000. **ⓦ** www.aval.ua/eng/

Central Post Office The place for stamps, mobile phone rentals and phone cards. **ⓐ** Slovatskoho 1. **ⓣ** (322) 721 080. **ⓦ** www.post.lviv.ua

Pavuk is an excellent internet café to help you keep in touch with those back home. It is located right by the main bus stop on Svobody. **ⓐ** Svobody prospekt 7.

TAKING A BREAK

Bar Mlecnzy The name means 'Milk Bar' and down-home, farm-fresh goodies are what to expect. Join the locals and enjoy a snack in this unpretentious little place just around the corner from the Potocki Palace. **ⓐ** Kopernika 9. **ⓛ** Daily 19.00–20.00.

Celentano This pizzeria takes its name from the legendary Celentano brothers, who were local pizza tycoons back in the 1950s. Located just around the corner from the opera house, this is a great place to have lunch. You can create your own masterpiece by picking out the various toppings that take your fancy. ❷ Svobody prospekt. ❸ Daily 11.00–23.00.

New York Street Pizza A New York-themed pizzeria may not be your number one choice if you're coming in search of something out of the ordinary. But if you have had your fill of dumplings and goulash, or simply need a good salad, this is the place to try. The desserts are pretty good, too. ❷ Stefanyka 4. ❸ (322) 994 980. ❸ Daily 10.00–23.00.

Svit Kavy 'The World of Coffee' is just that – a compendium of the world's coffees under one roof. It is very upmarket in its style, with elegant polished wood furnishings. Set at the foot of the Latin Cathedral, it is a popular place with locals. ❷ Kathedralna ploscha 6. ❸ Daily 09.00–21.00.

❷ *There is much to see and do in Lviv's historic centre*

Tsukernia Serves up possibly the best desserts in all of Lviv, inside a cosy, old-world ambience. ❸ Staroyeveyska 3. 🕒 Daily 11.00–23.00

Viennese Café is an historic watering-hole that first opened in 1829. The chef here cooks up a host of classic Austro-Hungarian dishes. For a hearty snack, try the sausages with sauerkraut. If a coffee and a sweet are all you crave, you will have a truly Viennese choice. The café is just by the old Jesuit Church and on sunny days chairs fan out across the terrace onto Pidkovy ploscha. ❸ Svobody prospekt 12. ☎ (322) 722021. 🕒 Daily 09.00–22.00.

AFTER DARK

Restaurants
Vezha Kramariv HH Set in a restored medieval bastion on the fringe of Lviv's Old Town, this restaurant will have you feeling like a conquering invader as you tuck into a range of Ukrainian and European dishes. It is warm and cosy and has regular jazz concerts in the evening. A good place to get the flavour of old Lviv. ❸ Svobody prospekt 16. 🕒 Daily 17.00–23.00.

Grand Restaurant HHH When you hunger for a little old-world flair, head for the Grand Restaurant. The food is great and the staff are friendly and knowledgeable. The chef prepares a range of both local and international cuisine. Definitely the place for a sophisticated palate. ❸ Svobody prospekt 13. ☎ (322) 724 042. 🕒 Daily 07.00–24.00.

Bars, clubs & casinos
Dzyga Bar is hangout for artists and arty types at the northern end of the old Armenian street. It is truly atmospheric and very old-world.

In the summer have a seat outside and watch the world go by.
📍 Virmenska 35. 🕐 Daily 10.00–23.00.

Grand Club Casino If you feel like trying your luck on the gaming tables you can rub shoulders with the colourful characters who make up Ukraine's new business elite here at Lviv's smartest club. Besides classic roulette, poker and blackjack, there will also be dancing girls at weekends. You'll find the club next to the Switocz confectionery on Lviv's swishest pre-war street. 📍 Shevchenka prospekt 10. ☎ (322) 729 000. 🌐 www.ghgroup.com.ua/gc.htm 🕐 Daily 09.00–06.00.

Lialka is a place where you will hear pop to punk, hard metal to techno and almost everything in between. Locals favour the house speciality *salo v shokoladi* (lard in chocolate!).
📍 Havryshkevycha ploscha 1. 🕐 Daily 11.00–02.00.

Split is another of Lviv's many casinos. If you enjoy throwing your money away, this is one of the better places to do so. 📍 Mitskevich 6/7. ☎ (322) 987133. 🌐 www.split.lviv.ua 🕐 Daily 18.00–06.00.

Titanic Step inside this elegant old townhouse and you will find yourself in an uncompromisingly kitsch setup, where sea-dogs rule the roost. It has over-the-top decor, and even the bar resembles the porthole side of some gallant vessel. No matter that Lviv is about as far from the sea as you can be in Europe. 📍 Teatralna 4–6. ☎ (322) 975 521. 🕐 Daily 11.00–23.00.

ACCOMMODATION

George H–HH Combining a shabby-chic elegance with modern

conveniences, the Hotel George is centrally located in the heart of the old town. First-class rooms have TV, hairdryers, internet access and refrigerators. Second-class accommodation requires that you share a bathroom. However, a shared bathroom could be a small price to pay to sleep where Balzac, Jean-Paul Sartre and Liszt have all spent a night. ➌ Mitskavicha ploscha 1. ☎ (322) 275952. ⓦ www.lviv.uar.net/~geoh/index.htm

Dnister HH A hotel that has hosted such dignitaries as Hillary Clinton and several heads of state must be doing something right! It is located in the historic heart of the city and is a short 6 km (4 miles) from the airport and 3 km (2 miles) from the railway station. The atmosphere is delightfully dignified, very old-school European, with an abundance of modern amenities to keep 21st-century travellers satisfied. ➋ Matejka 6. ☎ (322) 971017. ⓦ www.dnister.lviv.ua

Hetman HH This reasonably priced accommodation has rooms equipped with colour TV and radio. The major drawbacks are that most rooms share a bath and the hotel is located outside the tourist old town area. Still, if pennies are tight, this is a sensible solution. ➌ Volodomyra Velykoho 50. ☎ (322) 649 981. ⓦ www.hetman.lviv.ua/en

Zamok Leva HH This moderately priced, clean and pleasant hotel is designed as a mock-castle. There are some very famous names scribbled in its register, including Mikhail Gorbachev and Victor Yushenko. The 'Lion's Castle' was home to a noble Austrian family in the early part of the 20th century and later housed Communist party bosses before Ukraine's independence. Services include email, television and fax. The most reasonably priced accommodation is in

the double rooms in the basement. ⓐ Hlinky 7. ❶ (322) 386116.
ⓦ www.lionscastle.com

Eney HH–HHH Situated in a quiet part of town near the University,
this is a small, very modern hotel. It resembles a small apartment
building, and with only 14 rooms available it would be wise to book
well in advance. Amenities include TV, minibar and wireless internet
services. Breakfast is included and children under the age of six stay
for free in the same room. ⓐ Shimzeriv 22. ❶ (322) 768799.
ⓦ www.eney.lviv.ua

Nton HH–HHH Opened in 2001 and situated about 3 km (2 miles)
from the centre of town, this hotel is quite a success story and has
become a bit of a haunt for Ukrainian and Russian film stars staying
in Lviv. It has grown from only 20 rooms when it opened to over 60
rooms and suites. The decor is simple and modern. Room prices
include breakfast. ⓐ Shevchenka prospekt 154 b. ❶ (322) 337172.
ⓦ www.hotelnton.lviv.ua

Volter HH–HHH The Nton's sister hotel opened in 2004. The smart
but simply decorated rooms are all equipped with TV, internet and
telephone. It's located about 3 km (2 miles) from the city centre.
ⓐ Lypynskoho 60a. ❶ (322) 948888.
ⓦ www.hotelnton.lviv.ua/volter/en/index.htm

Grand Hotel HHH This is the poshest place to stay in Lviv. Recently
renovated to reflect its 1898 *belle époque* grandeur, the hotel features
well appointed rooms, a health club with a beautiful indoor
swimming pool, restaurants, a casino and a staff who speak English.
ⓐ Svobody prospekt 13. ❶ (322) 724 042. ⓦ www.ghgroup.com.ua

Odessa

Odessa more than deserves its title of 'Pearl of the Black Sea'. This charming, raffish and sometimes elegant city is filled with distinctive architecture set along carefully planned 19th-century streets and boulevards. Catherine the Great once imagined that Odessa could become the St Petersburg of the South and encouraged immigrants to settle here. Russian, rather than Ukrainian, is its first language.

Because of its history and its role as a trading port, Odessa has grown into a cosmopolitan city, more Mediterranean in outlook than central European. You will discover the inhabitants to be cultured, stylish and savvy. No wonder its lively nightlife makes this city a popular weekend getaway for residents of Kiev. The sunny climate of the city has made it a favourite resort spot for decades. And although part of the city has definitely seen better days, it retains a lively chic.

Odessa will fill you with a sense of déjà vu, particularly if you have seen Sergei Eisenstein's classic film *Battleship Potemkin*, which makes use of the **Potemkin Steps** leading to the harbour from Primorksy bulvar. Odessa is mostly a Russian-speaking town, but most of the signage is in Ukrainian as well.

Getting from Kiev to Odessa is easy, with many options. The least expensive is to take the bus or the train. A bus costs less than 60Hr. one way and takes 8–11 hours, depending on weather and traffic conditions; the journey time should drop considerably if and when the new highway between Kiev and Odessa is completed. Train fares and journey times are comparable, and there are daily departures. One of the several daily internal flights between Kiev and Odessa will cost about 1000Hr. return and flight time is about 90 minutes.

SIGHTS & ATTRACTIONS

The architecture and general ambience, rather than specific sights, are the attractions of Odessa. The beaches are for more than just swimming; this is is where people head to see and be seen. The atmosphere is reminiscent of the Victorian English seaside, with its sideshows, cafés and bars. Closest to the city centre are Arkadia and Lanzheron beaches. Arkadia is the liveliest for hanging out, while Lanzheron has a more family-oriented atmosphere. Both beaches are crowded and dirty, and swimming is not recommended. The further south you travel the less busy, and cleaner, the beaches become. Delphin and Fontan beaches are both are clean and safe, even for children.

For a few years now a major cleanup effort has been taking place, and the local government declares all the beaches safe for

swimming. However, use your own judgement and if in doubt don't dive in.

If you are travelling with the kids and they get bored with the beach, Luna Park is a small amusement park with about a dozen rides:

Luna Park ❸ Novoshch-epnoi Ryad 27. Ilicha Park (behind Privoz bazaar). ❶ (482) 220966. ❷ Daily 11.00–24.00 May–Sept.

CULTURE

East & West Art Museum
Inside this quaint little palace fronted by four pale blue columns is a solid collection of Western European and Oriental art. The Western

● *The historic Potemkin Steps lead to Odessa's passenger ship terminal*

collection includes canvases by Italian, French and Dutch artists – the Italian collection is the most significant by far.

@ Pushkinskaya 9. ☎ (482) 228 490. ⏱ Daily 10.00–18.00.

Fine Arts Museum

Opened in 1899, the museum houses a modest collection of both European and Ukrainian art, from which most of the Soviet-era exhibits have been removed. The collection was enhanced by a donation of works from the St Petersburg Museum of Arts. There is also a rich collection of 15th- and 16th-century Russian icons.

@ Sofievskaya 5A. ☎ (482) 237287. ⏱ Wed–Mon 10.30–17.00.

Historic Defence of Odessa Museum

The museum is dedicated to the defenders of the city in World War II. Although the city fell to the Germans and Romanians in October 1941 after a heroic defence, the partisans continued to harass the occupiers until the city was freed in April 1944. The best part of the museum is outside the building. Tanks, anti-aircraft guns and even a submarine are on display. Inside the two-room museum are posters, pictures and small arms.

@ Dacha Kovalevskogo 150. ☎ (482) 444527. ⏱ Sat–Thur 10.00–17.30.

History & Local Lore Museum

This museum's collection spans the history of Odessa from the 14th century to the present. Exhibits include photographs, documents, money, military memorabilia and historic clothing. There is also a section titled 'Sister Cities' that shows the many international cities with which Odessa holds close ties.

@ Gavannaya 4. ☎ (482) 228490. ⏱ Sat–Thur 10.00–16.30.

Port Museum

This museum, comprising three exhibition halls, was opened in 1988 and details the history of the port of Odessa in photographs, maps and documents. A newly opened hall includes a 5 m (15 ft) model of the port. The daughter of the museum founder frequently gives tours in English for visitors. ⓐ Lanzheronovskaya spusk 2. ⓣ (482) 729 3857. ⓛ 10.00–17.00.

Musical & Comedy Theatre

This is currently home to the local opera company. The building is lovely but save your money for performances of the Philharmonic Orchestra.
ⓐ Panteleimonovskaya 3. ⓣ (482) 250924.

Philharmonic Theatre

Here you'll find the Odessa Philharmonic, the best regional orchestra of the former Soviet Union. Currently it is led by Hobart Earle, an American conductor, who was once a pupil of Leonard Bernstein. Unfortunately the orchestra does not play during the summer months.
ⓐ Bunina 15. ⓣ (482) 226349.

RETAIL THERAPY

Tovkuchka is Odessa's weekend flea market, a huge bazaar filled with all kinds of useful and useless stuff. Take the south-west-bound Tram 4 from Uspenska to the end of the line and then transfer to Bus 160. The central part of the market is on Privozna at the south-eastern end of Oleksandrivsky prospekt.

Deribasovskaya A little more traditional, this is Odessa's main commercial street, filled with all kinds of tacky souvenir stores. What to buy? Matreshka dolls, hand-painted wooden boxes, embroidery and Soviet-era pins and medals all make good souvenirs.

TAKING A BREAK

Anastasiya is an inexpensive eatery with a shady rooftop deck. The food is good but the preparation time can be lengthy.
🅰 Arkadia Beach. 🕐 Daily 24 hours.

Arabskaya Kuhnya is an authentic taste of Arabia in Odessa, inexpensive and quite popular with locals.
🅰 Staroportofrankovskaya 18. 📞 (482) 73208 21. 🕐 Daily 11.00–24.00.

Dva Karla is an excellent place for shashklik – chicken, pork or lamb. The portions are huge and the prices are low. This basement restaurant is surprisingly bright and cheerful. In summer you can eat on a shady terrace. 🅰 Gretcheskaya 32. 📞 (482) 247182. 🕐 Daily 13.00–24.00.

Panorama is possibly the most expensive and over-priced restaurant in the city. Why should you go? For the spectacular view! Located on the top floor of the Kempinski Hotel, this is a great place to go for an afternoon coffee and to drink in the splendid panorama.
🅰 Primorskaya 6. 📞 (482) 72948 08. 🕐 14.00–last client.

Top Sandwich This Mid-Eastern sandwich shop, part of a small chain of three restaurants, serves up falafel, hummus and shashlik. It is a good choice for vegetarians. The apple and orange juices are freshly

pressed and squeezed. 🄰 Preobrazhenskaya 52. 🕿 (482) 264332.
🕒 Daily 24 hours.

Zara Pizzara is a good spot for a breakfast, lunch or dinner. It is one
of the few places in Odessa with a salad bar. The pizza is great, too.
🄰 Rishelevskaya 5. 🕿 (482) 72888 88. 🕒 Daily 9.00–23.00.

AFTER DARK

Restaurants
Estrellita HH When you need a taste of the American Southwest,
this is the place to head for a burrito or margarita. Only a short
distance from Potomkin Square, this has to be one of the best Tex-
Mex restaurants in Ukraine. There is also live music most evenings.
🄰 Ekaterininskaya 1. 🕿 (482) 372920. 🕒 Daily 24 hours.

Kumanets HHH If prodigious portions of good Ukrainian food are
what you seek, you will find them at Kumanets. Red borscht, green
borscht, *vareniky* and *diruny* are all worth a try. You will need a
reservation for a weekend evening. 🄰 Gavannaya 7. 🕿 (482) 376946.
🕒 Daily 11.00–23.00.

Clubs & shows
Ibiza DJs and go-go dancers make this one of Odessa's more
'swinging' spots. It is a little retro, but lively. 🄰 Arkadia Beach.
🕿 (482) 777 0205. 🕒 Daily 24 hours, May–Sept.

Itaka This seaside amphitheatre hosts Russian pop artists and other
genres from time to time. 🄰 Arkadia Beach. 🕿 (482) 349188.
🕒 Daily 24 hours, May–Sept.

ACCOMMODATION

Hotels in Odessa grade themselves, so a three-star hotel in the city may not bear any comparison with a three-star hotel anywhere else in the world. The grading system tends to be based on physical space rather than amenities, and bad service or worn and neglected interiors don't count. If your wallet is really flat, the cheapest accommodation to be found is a room in someone's home. To find one, go to the station and look for a person, usually an older woman, with a sign reading **KOMHATA** (*komnata*, 'room'). Be sure to ask if hot water is available. The going rate is about 75–100Hr. a night.

Bristol HH The baroque-styled Hotel Bristol, former Krasnaya, was built in 1899 and is comfortable and well furnished. Rooms have TV, minibar, showers and telephones. Bristol. ⓐ 15 Pushkinskaya. ⓣ (482) 250338.

Chernoye More HH–HHH is located in the centre of Odessa, only a 10-minute walk from the railway station. It is also very close to one of the city beaches. Rooms are plain, but nice, and are equipped with a bath or shower, TV, minibar and telephone. ⓐ 59 Richelievskaya. ⓣ (482) 242028.

Londonskaya HH–HHH Odessa's oldest luxury hotel is definitely showing signs of age, but there is just enough Regency flair left to keep it a charming experience. Non-smoking rooms are available, and there is an excellent restaurant on site. ⓐ 11 Primorsky bulvar. ⓣ (482) 259362.

○ *Waiting room facilities are good at Kiev's modern railway station*

PRACTICAL information

Directory

GETTING THERE
By air
Kiev is served by most major airlines, flying from most major European cities. British Airways, Air France, Austrian Airlines, Delta, KLM and Lufthansa have regular flights there. The two airlines of Ukraine, Ukraine International Airlines and Aerosvit, also fly to most major European cities. Aerosvit also has a weekly flight to Toronto, and three flights a week to New York (JFK). Austrian Airlines has the most experience of flying into Ukraine, and many airlines connect with Austrian in Vienna. Contact numbers in Kiev for all of these airlines are given below.

British Airways ☎ 490 6060. Ⓦ www.ba.com
Air France ☎ 464 1010. Ⓦ www.airfrance.com
Austrian Airlines ☎ 230 0020. Ⓦ www. aua.com
Delta Airlines ☎ 246 5656. Ⓦ www.delta.com
KLM ☎ 44 490 2490. Ⓦ www.klm.com
Lufthansa ☎ 490 3800. Ⓦ www.lufthansa.com.
Ukraine International Airlines ☎ 461 5656. Ⓦ www.ukraine-international.com
Aerosvit ☎ 490 3490. Ⓦ www.aerosvit.com

By rail
The train service to Kiev from Western Europe is very good and connects through Berlin. A direct journey from the UK by rail will involve a cross-Channel ferry or the Eurostar to Brussels as the first leg of your journey. The monthly *Thomas Cook European Rail Timetable* has up-to-date schedules for train services to and within Ukraine.

Eurostar and German Railways link London with Berlin. The Berlin–Kyiv section takes just over a day, and costs about 700Hr. Those travelling by train will require a visa to transit Belarus.

Rail Europe www.raileurope.co.uk

Eurostar Reservations (UK) ☎ 08705 186186 🅦 www.eurostar.com

Thomas Cook European Rail Timetable ⓘ (UK) 01733 416477; (USA) 1 800 322 3834. 🅦 www.thomascookpublishing.com

Ukrainian rail information There is good information on the web at: www.seat61.com/ukraine.htm

Driving

Driving your own car into Ukraine is not recommended. To start with, few of the border guards speak English. On entry, you will have to sign papers promising to remove the car from the country within two months, which could prove difficult if your car is stolen or wrecked, which happens to a lot of cars with foreign licence plates. Automobile insurance is mandatory in Ukraine, as is an international driver's licence.

If you must drive to Kiev from Western Europe, it is easiest to follow Highway E-40, which runs from Brussels through Germany and Poland and into Ukraine, through Lviv and directly into Kiev. There are also good routes to Kiev from the former Eastern bloc countries that border Ukraine. Almost all lead to Kiev.

Speed limits are 60 kph (37 mph) in cities, 90 kph (56 mph) on secondary highways and 130 kph (80 mph) on main highways. There is zero tolerance for drinking and driving. Traffic police do not use breathalysers, just their noses, to determine if a driver has been drinking. If you are stopped for a traffic violation, you can expect to pay the fine (or make a 'donation') on the spot.

ENTRY & EXIT FORMALITIES

Visiting Ukraine as a tourist has been easier since visa requirements were greatly relaxed. Visitors from EU countries, Switzerland, Liechtenstein, Canada, USA and Japan no longer require visas to enter Ukraine if they are staying for 90 days or less. Visitors from all other countries, and all those wanting to stay longer, still need a visa, which can be obtained from any Ukrainian embassy or consulate. Visas are also still required for students, and for people doing business in the country.

On entry

On entering the country, you will not be required to fill out customs forms if you are bringing in less than the equivalent of 10,000Hr. in other currencies, and if you have no declarable goods. Otherwise, customs forms are available in English on flights into Ukraine, but are normally only available in Ukrainian at border crossings for cars, trains and buses. You are allowed to bring in 1 litre of alcohol or 2 litres of wine or 10 litres of beer, and 200 cigarettes. You are also limited to 1 kg (2 lb) of detergent. Prohibited items include illegal drugs, weapons, radioactive items, plants and animals. Certain types of propaganda, especially those promoting genocide, racial hatred and overthrow of the government, are also prohibited. You may be required to purchase medical insurance issued by the state when entering the country.

Customs

Customs and Immigration is still quite bureaucratic, with long queues, so expect to take up to an hour to clear. Be patient, you will get through. Most immigration officials at Boryspil Airport speak English, but few immigration officials at other border crossings do.

Be sure to keep your passport with you at all times, as you may be asked to present it at any time by the police. Also, keep the customs forms, as you will need to present these when leaving the country.

On exit

You can expect to have your passport checked and customs form reviewed before you leave Ukraine. There are restrictions on what you can take out of the country. It is forbidden to remove certain antiquities and icons from the country. There are also restrictions on the amount of local currency, alcohol and caviar that you can take out. Most reputable merchants are aware of the restrictions, so ask them before you buy these items.

WHAT TO TAKE

Kiev is one of those destinations where you won't want to pack lightly. Items that we consider readily available and easy to obtain may not be, even in the capital city. Some good things not to leave home without include good toilet paper, a multi-purpose knife (with a screwdriver head), hand sanitiser, flashlight (torch) and a sewing kit. A mini-medicine chest is a good idea, too, stocked with antiseptic cream, anti-diarrhoea pills, tummy settlers, nasal decongestant or favourite cold remedy, painkillers and plasters (band aids). If you wear contact lenses, make sure you have an adequate supply of cleaning solution. For the most part you should be able to buy your cosmetic needs in Kiev, but if you have particular favourites, take a supply along.

A small Ukrainian or Russian dictionary will be of great help (to supplement the phrases in the back of this book). *The Thomas Cook Eastern European Phrasebook* has a wide range of useful phrases in Ukrainian (and Russian, useful in Odessa). Take plenty of business

cards. Ukrainians are fond of these cards and take delight in the ritual exchange of them.

Don't be afraid to take your stylish clothing to Kiev. If ever there was a city that is a slave to fashion, Kiev is it. Residents always wear their best out in public and will expect you to do the same. People here dress for dinner, for a performance at a theatre and for social outings. If you are heading to Kiev in the winter, dress warmly, from the inside out. In temperatures that frequently drop to -30°C (-22°F) you will want some good thermal underwear, warm socks that rise as high as your knees, insulated waterproof boots, lined gloves and a warm hat that covers your ears – and a nice long scarf to wrap several times around your neck to keep out the cold wind. By contrast in summer, when the temperature and the humidity makes it steamy, you will also want to dress in layers that you can peel off and still keep a certain level of modesty. If you plan on travelling by overnight train, say to Odessa, don't forget to pack a pair of pyjamas or a tee-shirt and running pants. Sleeping *au naturel* is not socially acceptable.

Pack it all up in an unassuming bag. Although Ukrainians may dress well, and like the Norwegians will pay particular attention to the quality of your footwear, luggage is not an area in which you will want to stand out. A smart, good-looking, high-quality case is an invitation to a robbery. If you have choice, select hard-sided over soft, as the soft-sided cases can be slashed open.

MONEY

The official currency of Ukraine is the hryvnia (pronounced hryv-nya) and designated as Hr (or UAH in currency exchanges and banks). The

◀ *Summer evenings in the Ukraine can be as balmy as anywhere on the Med*

TRAVEL INSURANCE

However you book your city break, it is important to take out adequate personal travel insurance for the trip. For peace of mind the policy should give cover for medical expenses, loss, theft, repatriation, personal liability and cancellation expenses. If you are hiring a vehicle you should also check that you are appropriately insured and make sure that you take relevant insurance documents and your driving licence with you.

hryvnia is divided into 100 kopecks. Coins come in denominations of 1, 5, 10, 25 and 50 kopecks and 1Hr. Notes come in 1, 2, 5, 10, 20, 50 and 100Hr. denominations. The hryvnia is currently pegged at about 5.33Hr. to US$1. Use of currencies other than the hryvnia is frowned upon, and few merchants will take euros, pounds sterling or US dollars.

It will be necessary to buy some hryvnia upon arrival, as it is virtually impossible to obtain the currency outside the country. When you exchange money, make sure the notes you are changing are in good condition, as most money changers will not accept tattered or torn notes or any that are not of the issuing country's latest design. Most hotels offer currency exchange and you can find currency exchange kiosks on major streets, so you should shop around a bit to get the best exchange rate.

ATMs, or Bankomats as they are locally known, are abundant, and the best way to manage your money in Kiev is to take it out in hryvnia from an ATM when you need it. Exchange rates are generally as good as or better than those at exchange offices and kiosks.

Some banks and ATMs may restrict the amount of cash you can withdraw. It should be noted that visitors are not permitted to leave the country with more than 85Hr. in cash.

Major credit cards are readily accepted by most major hotels, many restaurants, and some shops. However, it is wise to always carry some cash in case you find a merchant who will not accept them. Traveller's cheques, however, are not normally accepted, and should be avoided. A few banks will take them, but normally only in US dollars; cashing them can be lengthy and difficult, and you will be charged at least 2 per cent commission.

HEALTH, SAFETY & CRIME

Good travel insurance covering medical problems, personal injury and loss of property is an absolute essential for all trips to Kiev.

Do not drink the water. The water supply and sewerage systems in Kiev are in very bad shape, so not only do not drink the water, do not brush your teeth with it either, and avoid ice cubes in drinks unless you know that they have been made with clean or boiled water. Good mineral water is available everywhere, and at reasonable prices, so there is no reason to drink tap water. Despite precautions, many visitors do develop diarrhoea ('Gorbachev Gallop' in this part of the world), so bring along an anti-diarrhoea drug such as Imodium-D. If you do catch a bug, take the medicine, drink lots of fluids and wait it out. It should clear up in 24 hours. If it does not, it is time to get medical help.

Visitors should make sure that their immunisation shots are up to date, and those planning to go to a wooded area outside the city should be immunised against tickborne encephalitis. Although pharmacies are abundant in Kiev and are well stocked with medicines and other supplies, you should bring your own prescription drugs (in their original container), and, if required, your own sterile syringes.

Smoking

To date, there are no regulations against smoking in Ukraine, and you can expect a lot of second-hand smoke in just about any restaurant or bar, although some now offer no-smoking sections. Cigarettes for those that want them, are sold everywhere, and are very inexpensive.

Radiation

No one can forget the Chernobyl disaster. Fortunately for today's visitors, most of the radioactive cloud blew north and west, away from Kiev, although some radioactivity did reach the city. Today, radiation levels have dropped to normal, and visitors have nothing to fear. Day trips to the Chernobyl site are one of the more popular tourist attractions, and the higher radiation levels at Chernobyl are not considered dangerous if you do not stay too long. Nevertheless, Chernobyl is closed to under-18s and may not be an advisable destination for pregnant women.

Crime

Although organised crime is still a problem in Ukraine, the organised criminals tend to leave the tourists alone as long as the tourists do not interfere in the criminals' business. Crime against visitors is about average for large European cities. It is virtually impossible for foreigners to 'blend into' the local scene, so you can easily be a target for pickpockets, muggers and purse snatchers.

Take the normal precautions against crime when in Kiev. Do not flash expensive jewellery, large amounts of cash, or exhibit other signs of wealth. Try to use ATMs that are inside banks, and be mindful of people watching as you withdraw cash. Crowded areas, such as bus and railway stations, and busy markets should be avoided, as they are magnets for petty criminals. Do not carry bags of goods onto crowded buses and trams, as you may find the bag slashed and the goods gone. If possible, do not travel alone, especially at night, and especially if you have been drinking.

Cars should be locked and parked in open or well lit areas, with any valuables such as jewellery, cameras, mobile phones and computers locked in the trunk or otherwise out of sight.

OPENING HOURS

The official working week is Mon–Fri 09.00–17.00, although some offices work 10.00–18.00. Many offices still close for lunch 13.00–14.00. Some banks close early at 16.50. Bigger shops stay open later, until 20.00 or 21.00, seven days a week. Restaurants tend to open at noon and stay open until 23.00. Cafés and cafeterias open earlier, 08.00–09.00, and many close at 18.00 or 19.00. Museum hours are 09.00–17.00, although some stay open until 18.00. Most museums close two days a week, although the days vary, and some close during the last week of the month for cleaning.

TOILETS

Public toilets are generally nasty in Kiev. Many are of the old hole-in-the-floor type. Most also charge up to 50 kopecks to use. The better ones can be found at the new central railway station and in underground shopping centres. The worst are found in public parks and beaches. The toilets in fast-food restaurants, such as McDonald's, are normally good, but can deteriorate as the day goes on because of very high traffic.

CHILDREN

Bringing children, especially very young ones, to Kiev is not recommended. Dealing with the bureaucracy and worrying about drinking water and dirty toilets are made much worse with children in tow. Furthermore, few of the attractions in Kiev are of any interest to children.

COMMUNICATIONS

Phones

The telephone system is quite archaic, can be difficult to deal with, and sometimes does not work at all. The country code for Ukraine is 380, and the city code for Kiev is 44. When making a local call within Kiev, you can drop the city code, and just dial the seven-digit number (none of the Kiev numbers in this book includes the city code, but those for Lviv and Odessa do). Some public phones, if you can find one that works, will take a 50 kopeck piece, but most now require a UTEL card, which is available at any post office. Most post offices also have international phone booths, but an advance deposit is required, with the balance returned at the end of the call.

When calling outside the country, dial 8, wait for the tone, then dial 10 followed by the country code and the rest of the number. The country code for Australia is 61, the UK 44, the Republic of Ireland 353, South Africa 27, New Zealand 64, USA and Canada 1. If you need assistance making a call, an English-speaking operator can be reached by dialling 8 192. Long-distance rates are equivalent to about €1 per minute to Western Europe, or about €2.5 per minute to North America.

Most European mobile phones will work in Kiev. It is possible to

⊙ *Post offices usually also offer an ATM, and phone and fax facilities*

buy a Ukrainian chip if you are making a lot of calls – many mobile phone stores sell these – or to rent a mobile during your stay.

Post

Kiev's Central Post Office is located in the centre of the city on the Maidan Nezalezhnosti. It is huge and usually busy. Besides regular postal services, there are an internet café, fax services and international telephones. There are over 200 post offices in Kiev, so finding one should not be a problem. Just ask for 'de poshta'. Postboxes are hung on buildings throughout the city; they are yellow with the dark blue Cyrillic letters ПОШТА.

Although outgoing mail is slow, it is quite reliable. Incoming mail is not reliable, and it is better to use email or couriers such as FedEx and DHL. Outgoing mail should be sent airmail, and international postcards need to be placed inside an envelope. Letters to Europe take about ten days; letters to North America take two to three weeks. International letters cost about 3Hr. to mail. International mail can be addressed in Latin characters, but if possible repeat the destination country in Cyrillic characters (ask your hotel for help).

Central Post Office @ Khreschatyk 22. ❶ 228 1291. ❷ Mon–Sat 09.00–18.00.

Federal Express @ Kikvidze 44. ❶ 495 2020. ❷ Mon–Sat 09.00–19.00.

DHL @ Vasilkovskaya 1. ❶ 490 2600. ❷ Mon–Fri 08.00–20.00, Sat 09.00–16.00.

Internet

Internet access is not a problem in Kiev, although some of the servers can be erratic. Most of the better hotels now have business centres with internet access. The central post office has an excellent internet café on the second floor, and there are many internet cafés scattered throughout the city, including:

Bunker Computer Club ⓐ Artema 11a. ⓣ 212 4860. ⓛ Daily 24 hours.
Cyber Café ⓐ Prorizna 21. ⓣ 278 0548. ⓛ 00.00–24.00.
Pentagon Internet Bar ⓐ Khreschatyk 15. ⓣ 278 2182.

MEDIA

English-language newspapers and magazines are available in Kiev. The *Kiev Post* (ⓦ www.kyivpost.com) gives good, reliable information on everything from politics to entertainment. *What's On* (ⓦ www.whatson-kiev.com) provides up-to-the-minute information on restaurants, nightlife, entertainment and special events. Both of these publications, as well as imported English-language newspapers and magazines, are available at most major hotels, many newsstands, and at English-language bookstores.

ELECTRICITY

The standard is 220 V, 50 Hz. Most sockets use the standard continental European plug with 2 round pins; UK visitors will need a converter, North Americans a transformer as well, to use their appliances in Ukraine.

TRAVELLERS WITH DISABILITIES

Kiev is not user-friendly to those with mobility problems, although this is slowly changing. Steps are steep and curbs are high. The central railway station does have lifts for wheelchairs, but the rest of the public transit system does not have anything to aid accessibility. Some hotels and restaurants, however, do have facilities for travellers with disabilities. For information in your own country, contact:

Holiday Care UK-based advice. ☎ 0845 124 9971 .
Ⓦ www.holidaycare.org.uk
Tripscope Another useful source for UK travellers. ✉ Alexandra
House, Albany Road, Brentford, Middlesex TW8 0NE.
☎ 0845 758 5641. Ⓦ www.tripscope.org.uk
Irish Wheelchair Association ✉ Blackheath Drive, Clontarf, Dublin 3.
☎ (01) 818 6400. Ⓦ www.iwa.ie
Society for the Advancement of Travelers with Handicaps (SATH)
North American-based travellers. ✉ 347 5th Avenue, New York, NY
10016, USA. ☎ (212) 447 7284. Ⓦ www.sath.org
Access-able Ⓦ www.access-able.com
Australian Council for Rehabilitation of the Disabled (ACROD)
✉ PO Box 60, Curtin, ACT 2605; Suite 103, 1st Floor, 1–5 Commercial
Road, Kings Grove, 2208. ☎ (02) 6282 4333. Ⓦ www.acrod.org.au
Disabled Persons Assembly For New Zealand-based travellers.
✉ 4/173–175 Victoria Street, Wellington, New Zealand.
☎ (04) 801 9100. Ⓦ www.dpa.org.nz

FURTHER INFORMATION

Neither Ukraine nor Kiev has any organised tourist offices or official
tourist information, certainly not in English. Many hotels in Kiev,
however, do have details available in English and tour companies'
websites (see opposite) are often a good source of information.
Ukrainian embassies abroad do have some information, but it is
poor, with very little in English.

Information on the web

The following websites contain much useful information about
Kiev:

Ⓦ www.kiev-service.com has good information on hotels and apartments.

Ⓦ www.ukraininfo.com for information on flights to and accommodation in Kiev.

Ⓦ www.uazone.net/kiev is a very complete guide to the city, including hotels, attractions, car rentals, tours, shopping and restaurants

Ukraine-based tour companies

Kiev is one of those destinations where even an independent traveller will find that organised sightseeing can be a good way of experiencing a lot in a short time. The following companies Kiev-based unless otherwise stated) can be recommended.

SAM The leading tour operator in Ukraine; can arrange cruises, excursions and hotel bookings. Ⓐ Ivana Franka 40B. ⓣ 238 6959. Ⓦ www.sam.com

Mandrivnyk offer cruises, city tours and bus tours through Ukraine. If you have enough money, they can even arrange for a flight in a MiG. Ⓐ Poshtova ploscha 3. ⓣ 463 7604. Ⓦ www.mandrivnyk.com.ua

New Logic offers a full range of packages, hotel bookings, and theatre tickets. It caters to a younger crowd. Ⓐ Mykhaylivska 6A. ⓣ 206 3322. Ⓦ www.newlogic.com.ua

Meest-Tour specialises in adventure tours and hiking trips. Based in Lviv, it also has offices in Canada and the USA. Ⓐ Shevchenka 23, Lviv. ⓣ (32) 272 8710. Ⓦ www.meest-tour.com

Useful phrases

Ukrainian, a Slavonic language closely related to Russian, uses the Cyrillic alphabet. Outside tourist attractions and hotels, English is rarely spoken.

English	Ukrainian	Approx. pronunciation
BASICS		
Yes	Так	Tak
No	Ні	Ni
Please	Будь ласка	Bud' laska
Thank you	Дякую	Dyakuyu
Hello	Здрастуйте/Привіт	Zdrastuite/Pryvit
Goodbye	До побачення	Do pobachenya
Excuse me	Перепрошую	Pareproshuii
Sorry	Вибачте	Vybachte
That's okay	Все гаразд	Vse garazd
To	До, У	Do, U
From	З, Від	Z, Vid
Do you speak English?	Ви розмовляєте по-англійськи?	Vy rozmovlyaite po-anglyis'ky?
Good morning	Доброго ранку	Dobroho ranku
Good afternoon	Добрий день	Dobryi den'
Good evening	Добрий вечір	Dobryi vechir
Goodnight	На добраніч	Na dobranich
My name is ...	Мене звуть ...	Mene zvitj ...
DAYS & TIMES		
Monday	Понеділок	Ponedilok
Tuesday	Вівторок	Vivtorok
Wednesday	Середа	Sereda
Thursday	Четвер	Chetver
Friday	П'ятниця	P'yatnytsa
Saturday	Субота	Subota
Sunday	Неділя	Nedilya
Morning	Ранок	Ranok
Afternoon	День	Den'
Night	Ніч	Nich
Yesterday	Вчора	Vchora
Today	Сьогодні	Syogodni

English	Ukrainian	Approx. pronunciation
Tomorrow	Завтра	Zavtra
What time is it?	Котра година?	Kotra hodyna?
It is ...	Зараз ...	Zaraz ...
09.00	Дев'ять годин	Dev'yat' hodyn
Midday	Полудень	Poludenya
Midnight	Північ	Pivnich

NUMBERS

One	Один	Odyn
Two	Два	Dva
Three	Три	Try
Four	Чотири	Chotyry
Five	П'ять	P'yat'
Six	Шість	Shyst'
Seven	Сім	Sim
Eight	Вісім	Visim
Nine	Дев'ять	Devyat'
Ten	Десять	Desyat'
Twenty	Двадцять	Dvatsyat'
Fifty	П'ятдесят	P'yatdesyat
One hundred	Сто	Sto
One thousand	Тисяча	Tysyacha

MONEY

I would like to change these traveller's cheques/this currency	Я хотів би обміняти дорожні чеки/ цю валюту	Ya hotiv by obminyaty dorojni checky/ tsyu valiutu
Where is the nearest ATM?	Де знаходиться найближчий банкомат?	De znakhoditsja najblizhchi bankomat?
Do you accept credit cards	Ви приймаєте кредитні картки?	Vy pryimaete credytni kartky?

SIGNS & NOTICES

Airport	Аеропорт	Aeroport
Smoking/ non-smoking	Місце для паління/ Не палити	Mistse dlya palinnya/ Ne palyty
Platform	Платформа	Platforma
Toilets	Туалети	Tualety
Ladies/Gentlemen	Жіночий/Чоловічий	Zhinochyi/Cholovichyi
Underground (Subway)	Метро	Metro

Emergencies

EMERGENCY PHONE NUMBERS
Fire ☎ 01
Police ☎ 02
Ambulance ☎ 03

HOSPITALS
Most local hospitals should be avoided if possible. The following are
Western-standard hospitals that are open 24 hours a day.
American Medical Centre is considered the best in Kiev at present.
ⓐ Berdychivska 1. ☎ 490 7600. ⓦ www.amcentres.com
Boris Clinic ⓐ Velyka Vasylkivska 55a. ☎ 238 0000.
ⓦ www.boris.kiev.ua
Medikom is Ukraine's first private medical company. ⓐ Kondratyuka
8. ☎ 432 8888. ⓦ www.medicom.kiev.ua
Ukrainian-German Clinic ⓐ Chervonoarmiyska 67/7. ☎ 220 5572.
ⓦ www.unk.kiev.ua

PHARMACIES
Pharmacies are easy to find in Kiev – easily identifiable by their
standard green and white colour scheme. The following are open 24
hours.
VO Pharmacia (City Centre) ⓐ Moskovoska 2. ☎ 573 8708.
VO Pharmacia (Podil) ⓐ Verkhny Val 48. ☎ 463 7028.
VO Pharmacia (Left Bank) ⓐ Raisy Okipnoy 2. ☎ 516 2177.

POLICE
If you are a victim of crime, try to avoid going directly to the police.
At present, the locals have very little respect for the police, and for

good reason. Many police officers are thought to be corrupt, and few of them are fluent in English. Soviet-style bureaucracy still pervades law enforcement. Present your problem to your hotel management, or to your tour operator if you are on a package holiday. They can probably help with the proper authorities, and cut through the red tape. Only go to the police as a last resort, or if the crime is serious.

EMBASSIES & CONSULATES

Australian Embassy 🏛 Kominternu 18, Apt 11. ☎ 235 7586. 🌐 www.embassy.gov.au/ua.html 🚇 Metro: Vokzalna.

British Embassy 🏛 Desiatynna 9. ☎ 490 3600. 🌐 www.britemb-ukraine.net

Canadian Embassy 🏛 Yaroslaviv Val 31. ☎ 464 1144. 🌐 www.kyiv.gc.ca 🚇 Metro: Zoloti Vorota.

US Embassy 🏛 Kotsyubynskoho 10. ☎ 490 0000. 🌐 www.usemb.kiev.ua

---

EMERGENCY PHRASES

Help! Допоможіть! *Dopomozhit'!*

Call an ambulance/a doctor/the police/the fire brigade!
Викличте швидку/лікаря/міліцію/пожежних!
Vyklychte shvydku/likarya/ militsiyu/pozhezhnyh!

Can you help me please?
Ви не могли б мені допомогти, будь ласка?
Vi ne mogli b meni dopomogti, bud' laska?

A

accommodation 44–49
activities 43
air travel 138
airport 58–59
Andrew's Descent 73–74
Andriivsky uzviz 73–74
annual celebrations 10–12
ATMs 144–145

B

Babi Yar 108–110
babushkas 30
Bald Mountain of
    Vydubichi 15
ballet 40
Bandanelli Palace
    Museum, Lviv 118
bars & clubs 39–40
    central Kiev 87
    Lviv 124–125
    Odessa 135
    Podil 106
beaches 130
Bila Tserkva 114
bus station 60

C

cafés
    central Kiev 82–84
    Lviv   122–123
    Odessa 134–135
    Pechersk 98
    Podil 104–105
car hire 68
casinos 40
    central Kiev 88
    Lviv 124
Caves Monastery 90–96
CCA 103–104
Central Botanical
    Gardens 97
central railway station 44,
    59–60
Chernobyl (Chornobyl) 47,
    112–113

Chernobyl National
    Museum, Podil 100–103
children 148
Church of the
    Assumption 94
cinemas 89
classic music 40–41
    central Kiev 88–89
climate 8
Cossacks 17
credit cards 145
crime 146
culture 22–26
currency 143–144
customs regulations
    140–141

D

Desiatynna Church 74
Diakova 14–15
disabilities, travellers
    with 151–152
Dormition Cathedral 94
drinks 36
driving 60–61, 139
Dzyga Cultural Museum,
    Lviv 120

E

East & West Art
    Museum, Odessa
    130–132
electricity 151
embassies & consulates
    157
emergencies 156–157
entertainment 38–41
etiquette 21
events 12–13

F

festivals 10–12
Fine Arts Museum,
    Odessa 132
Folk Architecture & Life
    Museum, Pyrohovo 110
folk music 22–23

food & drink 32–37
funicular railway 100

G

Golden Gate 76

H

health 145, 156
Historic Defence of
    Odessa Museum 132
Historical Museum, Lviv
    118–120
history 16
History & Local Lore
    Museum, Odessa 132
hospitals 156
hostels 49
hotels
    Kiev 44–49
    Lviv 125–127
    Odessa 136
House with Chimeras 15,
    76

I

insurance 143
internet cafés 150–151

J

Jewish Kiev 109

K

Khreschatyk vulitsia
    70–72
Kiev Days 12–13
Kiev International Film
    Festival 13
Kievo-Pecherska Lavra
    90–96
Kontraktova ploscha 103

L

language 154–155
Lenin statue 76
lifestyle 18–21
listings media 151
Lviv Gallery of Art 120
Lviv Opera House 120

M

Maidan Nezalezhnosti 70
Marinsky Palace 72–73
Marionette Theatre 104
Market Square, Lviv
116–118
markets 30, 114
marshrutka 68
Molodist 13
Museum of One Street
103
Museum of Russian Art
78
Museum of the Great
Patriotic War 97
Musical & Comedy
Theatre, Odessa 133
Mykhaylivska
Zolotoverkhyi
Monasterya 75

N

National Art Museum 78
National History
Museum 76–77
National Museum of
Chernobyl, Podil
100–103
National Opera and
Ballet Theatre 78
National Parliament 72
nightlife 38–41
central Kiev 84–89
Lviv 124–125
Odessa 135
Podil 105–106

O

Odessa 128–130
opening hours 147

P

packing 141–143
passports & visas 140–141
Pereyaslav Khmelnytsky
114

pharmacies 156
Pharmacy Museum, Lviv
121
Philharmonic Theatre,
Odessa 133
phones 148–150
Podil Drama Theatre 104
Pokrovska Convent 110
police 156–157
poltergeists 14–15
Port Museum, Odessa
132–133
post 150
public holidays 13
public transport 64–68
puppet theatres 41, 104
Pyrohovo Museum of Folk
Architecture and Life
110

R

radiation 146–147
rail travel 138–139
railway station 44, 59–60
restaurants 34–36
central Kiev 85
Lviv 124
Odessa 135
Pechersk 98
Podil 105–106
Richard's Castle 14
Royal Mansion, Lviv
118–120
Russian Art Museum 78
Rynok ploscha, Lviv
116–118

S

safety 145–146
St Andrew legend 74
St Andrew's Church 74
St Michael's Golden-
Domed Monastery 75
St Nikolai's cathedral 112
St Sophia's Cathedral 75

St Vladimir's Cathedral
74–75
seasons 8
Shevchenko National
Opera and Ballet
Theatre 78, 88
Shevchenko, Taras 26
shopping 28–31
central Kiev 79–82
Kiev outskirts 114
Lviv 121–122
Odessa 133–134
Pechersk 98
smoking 146
Sofiysky Sobor 75
Soros Center of
Contemporary Art
103–104
sport 42–43

T

taxis 68
tickets 41
time differences 58
tipping 37
toilets 147
tour companies 153
tourist information
152–153
Trinity Gate Church 94
Troitskaya Church 94

V

Verkhovna Rada 72
Vydubytsky Monastery
97–98
Vydubichi 15

W

weather 8

Y

youth hostels 49

Z

Zoloti Vorota 76

The publishers would like to thank the following for supplying their copyright photographs for this book.

Tony Gervis: all images except
A1 pix: pages 49, 92, 102, 119, 126, 130 and 142.

Proofreader: Jan McCann
Copy editor: Stephen York

Send your thoughts to
books@thomascook.com

- **Found a great bar, club, shop or must-see sight that we don't feature?**

- **Like to tip us off about any information that needs a little updating?**

- **Want to tell us what you love about this handy little guidebook and more importantly how we can make it even handier?**

Then here's your chance to tell all! Send us ideas, discoveries and recommendations today and then look out for your valuable input in the next edition of this title. As an extra 'thank you' from Thomas Cook Publishing, you'll be automatically entered into our exciting monthly prize draw.

Email the above address (stating the title) or write to:
CitySpots Project Editor, Thomas Cook Publishing, PO Box 227, Unit 15/16, Coningsby Road, Peterborough PE3 8SB, UK.